M000300417

Creating Healing
School Communities

Concise Guides on Trauma Care Series

Creating Healing School Communities

School-Based Interventions for Students Exposed to Trauma

Catherine DeCarlo Santiago,
Tali Raviv, and Lisa H. Jaycox

AMERICAN PSYCHOLOGICAL ASSOCIATION
Washington, DC

Copyright © 2018 by the American Psychological Association. All rights reserved. Except as permitted under the United States Copyright Act of 1976, no part of this publication may be reproduced or distributed in any form or by any means, including, but not limited to, the process of scanning and digitization, or stored in a database or retrieval system, without the prior written permission of the publisher.

The opinions and statements published are the responsibility of the authors, and such opinions and statements do not necessarily represent the policies of the American Psychological Association.

Published by
American Psychological Association
750 First Street, NE
Washington, DC 20002
www.apa.org

APA Order Department
P.O. Box 92984
Washington, DC 20090-2984
Phone: (800) 374-2721; Direct: (202) 336-5510
Fax: (202) 336-5502; TDD/TTY: (202) 336-6123
Online: http://www.apa.org/pubs/books
E-mail: order@apa.org

In the U.K., Europe, Africa, and the Middle East, copies may be ordered from
Eurospan Group
c/o Turpin Distribution
Pegasus Drive
Stratton Business Park
Biggleswade Bedfordshire
SG18 8TQ United Kingdom
Phone: +44 (0) 1767 604972
Fax: +44 (0) 1767 601640
Online: https://www.eurospanbookstore.com/apa
E-mail: eurospan@turpin-distribution.com

Typeset in Minion by Circle Graphics, Inc., Columbia, MD

Printer: Edwards Brothers Malloy, Ann Arbor, MI
Cover Designer: Mercury Publishing Services, Inc., Rockville, MD

Library of Congress Cataloging-in-Publication Data
Names: Santiago, Catherine DeCarlo, author. | Raviv, Tali, author. | Jaycox, Lisa, author.
Title: Creating healing school communities : school-based interventions for students exposed to trauma / Catherine DeCarlo Santiago, Tali Raviv, and Lisa H. Jaycox.
Description: First edition | Washington, DC : American Psychological Association, [2018] | Series: Concise guides on trauma care book series | Includes bibliographical references and index.
Identifiers: LCCN 2017031131| ISBN 9781433828621 | ISBN 1433828626
Subjects: LCSH: School children--Mental health services. | Psychic trauma in children. | Post-traumatic stress disorder in children. | Counseling in education.
Classification: LCC LB3430 .S27 2018 | DDC 371.7/13--dc23
LC record available at https://lccn.loc.gov/2017031131

British Library Cataloguing-in-Publication Data
A CIP record is available from the British Library.

Printed in the United States of America
First Edition

http://dx.doi.org/10.1037/0000072-000

10 9 8 7 6 5 4 3 2 1

We dedicate this book to students facing adversities
and hope that it might help make schools supportive and healing
environments, so that you can learn and thrive.

Contents

CONTENTS

Series Foreword

Exposure to traumatic events is all too common, increasing the risk for a range of significant mental problems, such as posttraumatic stress disorder (PTSD) and depression; physical health problems; negative health behaviors, such as smoking and excessive alcohol consumption; impaired social and occupational functioning; and overall lower quality of life. As mass traumas (e.g., September 11, military engagements in Iraq and Afghanistan, natural disasters such as Hurricane Katrina) have propelled trauma into a brighter public spotlight, the number of trauma survivors seeking services for mental health consequences will likely increase. Yet despite the far-ranging consequences of trauma and the high rates of exposure, relatively little emphasis is placed on trauma education in undergraduate and graduate training programs for mental health service providers in the United States. Calls for action have appeared in *Psychological Trauma: Theory, Research, Practice, and Policy* with such articles as "The Need for Inclusion of Psychological Trauma in the Professional Curriculum: A Call to Action" by Christine A. Courtois and Steven N. Gold (2009) and "The Art and Science of Trauma-Focused Training and Education" by Anne P. DePrince and Elana Newman (2011). The lack of education in the assessment and treatment of trauma-related distress and associated clinical issues at undergraduate and graduate levels increases the urgency to develop effective trauma resources for students as well as postgraduate professionals.

The Concise Guides on Trauma Care series addresses that urgent need by providing truly translational books that bring the best of trauma psychology science to mental health professions working in diverse settings. To do so, the series focuses on what we know (and do not know) about specific trauma topics, with attention to how trauma psychology science translates to diverse populations (diversity broadly defined, in terms of development, ethnicity, socioeconomic status, sexual orientation, and so forth).

This series represents one of many efforts undertaken by Division 56 (Trauma Psychology) of the American Psychological Association to advance trauma training and education (e.g., see http://www.apatraumadivision. org/3/directory-resources-links.html). We are pleased to work with Division 56 and a volunteer editorial board to develop this series, which continues to move forward with the publication of this important guide by Catherine DeCarlo Santiago, Tali Raviv, and Lisa H. Jaycox on school-based interventions for students exposed to trauma. This volume offers a practical and accessible guide for how to infuse school systems with trauma-informed practices that would be beneficial to children and youth exposed to trauma. Improving schools' capacity to address the trauma-related mental health needs of students in order to support their learning and success is relevant to educators, school-based mental health providers, researchers, and policymakers alike. Santiago and colleagues integrate empirical information with practical implementation considerations while offering a useful overview of school-based prevention and intervention strategies. This practical book, grounded in scientific data, will be of great use to any professional working with children in the school system. Future books in the series will continue to address a range of assessment, treatment, and developmental issues in trauma-informed care.

Ann T. Chu
Anne P. DePrince
Series Editors

Foreword

Within schools across the United States, there are students who repeatedly challenge the adults in front of them. These challenges manifest in various ways, including verbal outbursts and aggression, refusal to engage in the learning environment, apathy, absenteeism, walking out of the classroom, and more. Some children push our buttons, sometimes over and over again. Naturally, this can cause us to question why we choose to work in schools, especially in schools that serve at-promise (formerly at-risk) students. Sometimes we leave work thinking, "What did I do to deserve that? What is wrong with these kids?" However, using a trauma lens encourages us to ask different questions, questions that push us to understand the lives of the students who present the greatest challenges to our practice. When we shift toward an effort to understand the underlying causes of students' unpredictable negative behaviors, we may uncover the layers of trauma that affect their lives.

Children exposed to trauma often bring complex needs and struggles to the classroom. Their negative behaviors have their roots in adverse and even horrific experiences. These traumatic experiences can leave behind scars that affect physical health, cognitive functioning, and relationships. The aftermath of being exposed to trauma shows up in students' behaviors and can cause unknowing educators to make assumptions about students, labeling them unruly, ungovernable, and disrespectful. These labels can undermine their receipt of needed supports.

Schools across the United States are charged with and pressured to raise the academic achievement of students, especially the achievement of struggling and vulnerable learners. Often, these struggling and vulnerable learners are highly concentrated in schools without the adequate resources to support them and without the additional incentives needed to recruit and retain high-performing, experienced teachers and staff. Given these conditions, the increased demands of implementing social–emotional learning and behavioral health supports can feel like "another thing" schools must do. Rather than an extra burden, we consider this a necessary and integral component of advancing academic achievement and personal outcomes for students.

Operating from a trauma lens has shifted the way we "do school." As the principal and assistant principal of an urban high school located on the South Side of Chicago, we recognize that our students are disproportionately exposed to violence and trauma. Our students are predominantly African American and Latino. Ninety-five percent of them are classified as low-income, and many of our students are experiencing housing mobility and food insecurity in addition to pervasive community and family violence and instability. When we became an administrative team in 2012, our school was designated as a "turnaround" school because of low academic performance. As a result, we focused heavily on teaching and learning—to a much greater extent than we focused on the behavioral health of our students. Behavioral health was a second tier solution in our multitiered approach. Tier one was centered on community building at the beginning of the school year and reactive discipline policies and structures in case students didn't comply with our rules. The problem with this approach is that we weren't spending time learning the history and complex stories that many of our students were living with day to day. All of our teaching strategies, curricula, tutorial programs, and special events couldn't heal the wounds with which our students were coming to school. We had to invest time in understanding our students' lives outside of school. As we studied adverse childhood experiences as a school community, we began to understand that students weren't "bad." They were stressed, struggling, and trying to cope with troubling situations beyond their control.

We believe that we are now building a school community where high-risk students can demonstrate high resilience. The process has involved adults demonstrating resilience by not quitting on students who struggle. Adults who are willing to engage in this work have to also give space and voice to their own reactions and vulnerabilities through intense learning, reflection, and forgiveness. As adults in our school make deeper connections with our students and families through empathy and ongoing support, we are seeing students rise out of their current struggle and enter college, giving themselves a shot at the middle class. Operating from a trauma-informed perspective isn't always easy. It's tough and messy work, and the necessary resources and interventions don't always exist. We believe that schools, especially those that serve vulnerable and high-risk students, must shift from focusing on reactive discipline strategies and policies to working with clinical staff and partners to create healing and supportive school climates, coupled with structures and processes that identify students who need mental health services to heal from their trauma and reach their full potential. We know this approach works because we have seen it transform hundreds of lives.

We have been lucky enough to partner and collaborate with leading experts to obtain training and consultation for our staff on the impact of trauma on students, to educate our staff on secondary traumatic stress, compassion fatigue and burnout, and to support us in the creation of behavioral health teams that identify struggling students and match them with the appropriate clinical interventions. Our district has invested in training school social workers and psychologists on evidence-based interventions, such as the Cognitive Behavioral Intervention for Trauma and Schools (CBITS), and we have had CBITS groups in our building offered annually. We have been fortunate to have community providers obtain their own grant funding to support them in providing Structured Psychotherapy for Adolescents Responding to Chronic Stress groups in our school (see Chapter 7 for more on these particular programs). We have seen the impact of these programs on our students, and we are proud of our ability to leverage our limited resources to invest in them. *Creating Healing School Communities: School-Based Interventions for Students Exposed to Trauma* is intended to provide clinicians working in schools with some of the tools necessary to bring these programs to their schools and to make progress along the path to creating their own healing school community. As you read this book, remember that you are a part of a larger movement whose mission is to provide mental health services to students who might not otherwise receive them. That's honorable. Best of luck to you.

Maurice R. Swinney
Principal

Ellen Kennedy
Assistant Principal
Tilden Career Community Academy
Chicago Public Schools

Acknowledgments

We gratefully acknowledge that this work builds on two decades of work within the Trauma Services Adaptation Center for Resiliency, Hope, and Wellness in Schools, part of the National Child Traumatic Stress Network.

Creating Healing
School Communities

Introduction

*K*enneth heard his name called and walked proudly across the stage. *As he accepted his diploma, he shared a smile with the school social worker who was sitting with the teachers. Few understood how meaningful this moment was, but she certainly had an idea. In middle school, Kenneth was fairly certain he would not graduate from high school and wondered if he would even make it to freshman year. On the verge of expulsion, Kenneth was struggling with behavior problems and depression stemming from a history of multiple traumas, including domestic violence and witnessing neighborhood violence. With the help of the school social worker, Kenneth learned to recognize his triggers and develop ways to calm himself in the moment. The school social worker supported Kenneth in asking his teachers for permission to step outside of the classroom when that was necessary to manage his anger. Over time, Kenneth became more open to sharing portions of his trauma history and ultimately chose to participate in a school-based trauma group with the*

http://dx.doi.org/10.1037/0000072-001
Creating Healing School Communities: School-Based Interventions for Students Exposed to Trauma, by C. D. Santiago, T. Raviv, and L. H. Jaycox
Copyright © 2018 by the American Psychological Association. All rights reserved.

encouragement of the social worker and a trusted teacher. Though Kenneth had been reluctant to join a group with other students, after participating, he realized how helpful it had been to see that other students had also experienced trauma and to feel accepted and supported in group. He felt connected to other students and found a safe space to both share his experiences and learn strategies for managing his anger and fears. Though Kenneth continued to struggle with anger and sadness periodically, he felt better able to focus on school and reach out to the social worker for support when needed. How can we help other students like Kenneth heal and reach their graduation day?

If you are a school mental health provider, you have probably worked with at least one student who has experienced trauma. Perhaps, like Kenneth, the trauma has affected the student's school performance and mental health. In this book, you will read about Kenneth and two other students whose stories demonstrate how trauma can manifest in students. You will also read about the best strategies available for supporting students like Kenneth. School mental health providers are tasked with the challenging job of supporting students with mental health needs in schools. The term *school mental health provider* is meant to refer broadly to school-based social workers, psychologists, counselors, and other clinicians who work within the school, including those who are employed directly by the school or school district and those who are employed by community agencies to provide services within schools.

This book provides a practical overview and guide for school mental health providers working with students who have been exposed to trauma. Our purposes are (a) to highlight the need for effective school-based interventions; (b) to review evidence-based interventions for trauma in schools; (c) to provide examples of the core treatment components of such interventions; and (d) to offer recommendations and strategies for successfully implementing these interventions in schools. Three levels of intervention strategies are discussed as is consistent with this Multi-Tiered System of Supports (MTSS) framework: Universal (Tier 1) strategies designed to improve outcomes for all students, Targeted (Tier 2) strategies aimed at selected students, and Intensive (Tier 3) interventions. The evidence for the effectiveness of interventions is reviewed. This book will guide school mental health providers in applying these interventions in their schools and in supporting educators and other school-based staff in creating classrooms and schools that are sensitive to the needs of students who have experienced trauma. Case vignettes help to illustrate the implementation of core treatment components. Furthermore, we review the common challenges that arise in the school context and suggest ways to overcome these barriers.

We begin with a review of trauma exposure among children and adolescents (Chapter 1) and the impact of this exposure on students' mental health, behavior, learning, and physical health (Chapter 2). In Chapter 3, we provide a rationale for school-based interventions highlighting how many students do not get treatment elsewhere. In Chapter 4, we review universal or schoolwide interventions that can support students exposed to trauma, including strategies for developing trauma-sensitive classrooms and schools. Chapter 5 discusses strategies that can be used by school mental health providers prior to implementing a targeted (Tier 2) intervention in their school, such as partnering with teachers and administrators and identifying students for intervention groups. Next, Chapter 6 summarizes the key components of evidence-based interventions, using case vignettes to illustrate how different skills may be implemented. Chapter 7 reviews Tier 2 and Tier 3 interventions for trauma in schools and the current level of evidence for such interventions. Finally, in Chapter 8, we highlight some of the common considerations and challenges faced by school mental health practitioners along with strategies for overcoming them. The resource list at the end of book summarizes useful websites, links, and sources of additional information. The numbered resources referenced in the text refer to items on the resource list.

As highlighted throughout this volume, implementing trauma interventions in schools can ensure that students receive needed treatment that they are unlikely to access outside of school. By receiving evidence-based support in schools, these students have the opportunity to heal from trauma. School-based supports can help minimize the impact that trauma can have on school functioning, while supporting the development of skills that help students manage current and future stress. Although work in schools can be extraordinarily rewarding, staff may also feel overwhelmed when trying to find the best ways to support students who have experienced trauma and stress. This book highlights some of the common challenges experienced by school mental health providers, offering strategies to employ before implementing a mental health intervention and describing special considerations for the school context. This book can help providers know where to start (if they have never implemented school-based trauma interventions before), and it offers additional strategies to enhance the efforts of experienced providers. We hope the material herein will guide and support school mental health providers as they engage in the important work of supporting students who have experienced trauma.

1

Trauma Exposure Among School-Aged Youth

In 2015, a landmark lawsuit was brought against a Southern California school district. The plaintiffs in the lawsuit were all high school students who had been exposed to significant trauma. These young people, all of whom had harrowing stories of abuse, neglect, exposure to violence, and homelessness, argued that they are entitled to the same rights and protections that students with physical, emotional, or learning disabilities are afforded under the Americans With Disabilities Act of 1990. The complaint filed in court alleged that the school district failed to meet the educational and mental health needs that resulted from exposure to trauma, responding to their behaviors and academic difficulties with punishment or disciplinary practices rather than support and services. In the face of the compelling stories of the individual plaintiffs, as well as the plethora of research on the impact of trauma on brain development and learning,

http://dx.doi.org/10.1037/0000072-002
Creating Healing School Communities: School-Based Interventions for Students Exposed to Trauma,
by C. D. Santiago, T. Raviv, and L. H. Jaycox
Copyright © 2018 by the American Psychological Association. All rights reserved.

a federal judge agreed with them (Resmovits, 2015). Although this was one lawsuit in one school district, it is a harbinger of the seismic changes occurring both in the domain of school mental health and the field of childhood trauma.

Our intention is to equip school mental health providers with the ethical and practical tools they need to support students, families, teachers and administrators—and indeed, the very ideal of education as a gateway to opportunity and social change.

STORIES OF CHILDREN AFFECTED BY TRAUMA

If you are reading this book, it is likely that you have encountered at least one student in your work who has made you want to learn more about what you could do to support him or her. Below are case study examples to help bring to life the experiences of the children in our nation's schools.

Eight-year-old William, a third-grader, was crossing the street with his mother and his two siblings when a car ran the stop sign, hitting his 4-year-old sister and dragging her underneath the car for half a block prior to driving off without stopping. William was knocked to the ground by the force of the impact and sustained minor cuts and scrapes. His mother and his 12-month-old brother were not injured. Subsequent to the accident, William witnessed his mother crying and screaming. He witnessed strangers running to their aid, with looks of shock and horror on their faces. He accompanied the ambulance to the emergency room, watching as the paramedics attempted to treat his sister. While still at the hospital, he learned that his sister had died in the accident. William attended his sister's funeral, witnessed his parents' grieving, and survived hundreds of reminders of his sister each day. Prior to this incident, William had not been exposed to significant stress or trauma.

Fifteen-year-old Sydnee, a high school sophomore, lived through a Category 4 hurricane. During the hurricane, Sydnee and her family had to evacuate to a local emergency shelter. On their way to the shelter, she witnessed the destruction of many homes in her neighborhood, cars floating in the streets, and bodies of injured and deceased people. Sydnee's family stayed in the shelter for days in crowded and unsanitary conditions with limited access to fresh food, water, and other necessities. While in the shelter, Sydnee was in contact with sick and injured individuals, crying babies, and fearful adults. She and her family had no contact during this time with relatives and friends, and they did not know whether loved ones were safe, injured, or even deceased. Prior to the hurricane, Sydnee and her family experienced the stress of living in poverty. Her parents both worked several jobs to support the family, and as the eldest in the family, Sydnee was responsible for helping to take care of younger siblings and the household. Despite this economic stress, they were a close-knit and supportive family who had strong relationships with extended family members and friends in their community.

Twelve-year-old Kenneth, a seventh grader, experienced multiple traumas throughout his life. As an infant and toddler, he was often woken by the sound of his parents arguing. His father was verbally and physically abusive to Kenneth's mother and to Kenneth himself. Police responded to calls at Kenneth's home on multiple occasions, often in the early hours of the morning. Kenneth also witnessed his father under the influence of drugs and alcohol and was often present as his father's friends and associates injected street drugs. Kenneth's father moved out of the home when Kenneth was 7 years old, and Kenneth had no contact with him since the age of 9. Over the years, Kenneth's mother struggled with depression. After his father left, his mother also often had difficulty paying the bills, and the family stayed with multiple different friends and family members, often sleeping on couches or the floor. As a result, Kenneth attended three different schools in 5 years. Their current home is in a violent neighborhood, where Kenneth and his friends witnessed gang-related violence, including a shooting that took place in the park across the street from his school.

WHAT IS TRAUMA?

Each of the students described in these case vignettes would be identified as having been exposed to one or more significant traumatic events, despite the significant variability in the incidents. The term *exposure to trauma* encompasses a myriad of scenarios, events, and circumstances. Trauma can consist of one or more episodes, or it can be chronic. It can be perpetrated by a person or it may result from an act of nature (e.g., hurricane, earthquake), or an accident that happens at random (e.g., bridge collapse). When perpetrated by a person, that person can be known to the victim (as in abuse or intimate partner violence), by a stranger (as in a home invasion), or by unknown persons removed from the victim (as in war or terrorism). At times, the perpetrator may even be causing trauma in an attempt to heal (as in trauma caused by medical procedures). The traumatic event may have been intentionally inflected by the perpetrator (as in assault) or may have been unintentional (as in a motor vehicle accident). The traumatic event may have been experienced directly, witnessed, or even relayed verbally to the child by others. One person, one family, several people, many families, or entire communities can be affected by the event. Despite the seemingly endless variations in the circumstances of trauma, what unifies these disparate events into a single concept is that the events cause intense fear, horror, or helplessness in those who experience, witness, or hear about them and may overwhelm the individual's ability to cope.

HOW COMMON IS EXPOSURE TO TRAUMATIC EVENTS AMONG CHILDREN AND YOUTH?

Trauma exposure is more common than most people realize, and as a result, educators and school mental health providers may not be aware of what students are bringing to school in their "invisible backpacks" each day. Although estimates of exposure vary based on children's ages, geographical location, types of traumatic event, and social variables, there is a general consensus in the field that exposure is likely the norm rather than the exception. For example, in one study conducted with a population sample of over 1,400 adolescents in western North Carolina, over two thirds of adolescents had experienced at least one traumatic event by their 16th birthday (Copeland, Keeler, Angold, & Costello, 2007). A national survey of adolescents replicated this finding, with 61.8% of 13- to 17-year-olds surveyed reporting at least one potentially traumatic event (McLaughlin et al., 2013). These studies assessed for exposure to a wide range of traumatic events, including interpersonal violence, accidents, man-made or natural disasters, life-threatening illness, the unexpected death of a loved one, and for knowing of a traumatic event occurring to a loved one.

Particular attention has been paid to exposure to violence in the home or community. In many schools and neighborhoods, exposure to violence nears epidemic proportions. Over two decades ago, for example, Bell and Jenkins (1993) conducted an exploratory survey of exposure to violence among 536 African American students at three Chicago-area elementary schools with shocking results: 26% of these 7- to 15-year-old children had witnessed a shooting and 30% had witnessed someone being stabbed. More recently, the U.S. Department of Justice and the Centers for Disease Control and Prevention jointly conduct the National Survey of Children's Exposure to Violence, a nationally representative epidemiological survey that assesses exposure to violence, crime, and abuse (that may or may not have been reported to authorities) for children from birth through age 17 (Finkelhor, Turner, Shattuck, & Hamby, 2015). Results from 2013–2014 were sobering: More than one third of youth experienced a physical assault during the preceding year, and almost a quarter of youth had witnessed violence in their family or community during that same time. Child abuse was also disturbingly prevalent: 38.1% of youth aged 14 to 17 had experienced maltreatment (including physical abuse, emotional abuse, and neglect) in their lifetimes, while 14.3% of girls and 6% of boys in this age range had experienced sexual assault. Finally, for many children surveyed, these were not isolated incidents: 40.9% of children had more than one direct experience of violence, crime, or abuse in a single year, and 10.1% of children had six or more direct experiences with violence.

WHO IS AT RISK FOR EXPERIENCING TRAUMA?

Children in Poverty

As demonstrated by the high rates of exposure to traumatic events just described, no segment of society is immune to the risk of exposure. However, risk of exposure is not equitably distributed among our nation's children, teenagers, schools, and communities. Children living in poverty are disproportionately at risk for living through a traumatic event, which occurs against a backdrop of chronic stress caused by living with less than one needs. Census data indicate that over one fifth of the nation's children live in poverty (DeNavas-Walt & Proctor, 2015), and many of these children live in neighborhoods where unemployment, residential mobility, and crime are the norm. Poor children are also more likely to experience family disruption and family violence (G. W. Evans, 2004). Even the likelihood of accidents and injuries is higher for poor children; these events are caused by increased street traffic, unsafe playgrounds, and the conditions in the very homes in which they reside, which are more likely to have inadequate heat, poor indoor air quality, structural problems, scalding tap water, and inadequate fire protections such as smoke detectors or fire extinguishers (G. W. Evans, 2004).

Ethnic Minority and Immigrant Youth

Rates of exposure to both familial violence and violence outside the home are higher for ethnic minority youth than for nonminority youth (Crouch, Hanson, Saunders, Kilpatrick, & Resnick, 2000). Ethnic minority youth are disproportionately represented among our nation's poor (American Psychological Association, n.d.), and they are also more likely to be living in densely populated urban environments; these conditions confer increased risk for traumatic exposure. However, the increased rates of exposure to violence among ethnic minority youth are not entirely explained by income disparities. Crouch and colleagues (2000) found that for Caucasian adolescents, the likelihood of being exposed to violence decreased as household income increased. However, the same was not true for African American and Hispanic youth, for whom increased household income was not associated with lower rates of violence exposure either within or outside of the home. The authors posited that continued segregation and discrimination may mean that increased income does not necessarily correspond with emergence out of dangerous neighborhoods for ethnic minority youth.

Children who have immigrated to the United States are also at higher risk for trauma exposure caused by factors other than poverty. For the nearly 2.8 million children born outside the United States (Child Trends, 2014), exposure to trauma may have occurred prior to migration to this country, during the process of migration, and after arrival. War, torture, terrorism, natural disaster, famine, poverty, social unrest, and violence are often among the reasons that individuals or families choose to migrate from their country of origin. The process of migration is also frequently dangerous and is almost always accompanied by loss of extended family and kinship ties (Pumariega, Rothe, & Pumariega, 2005). One study of more than 1,000 recent immigrants in Grades 3 through 8 showed that 88% of children had at least some exposure to violence in their lifetimes, with 49% reporting being victims of violence in the past year and 80% reporting witnessing violence in the past year (Jaycox et al., 2002).

Children With Disabilities

Within school settings, particular attention should be paid to children diagnosed with physical, emotional, or developmental disabilities. For example, one large study conducted with children enrolled in the Omaha Public Schools found that children with disabilities (as defined by the receipt of special education services) were over 3 times more likely to experience maltreatment than their nondisabled peers (Sullivan & Knutson, 2000), perhaps due in part to the elevated levels of stress that caring for a child with special needs may engender among parents and caregivers. Children with physical, emotional, or developmental disabilities are also at elevated risk for traumatic exposure other than child abuse, including peer victimization or bullying, sexual victimization, and property crime, although risk varies according to the type of disability and type of victimization (Turner, Vanderminden, Finkelhor, Hamby, & Shattuck, 2011). For example, children with poor social skills or differences in appearance or ability may be more likely to become targets of bullying. Risk of sexual victimization is thought to be heightened because of increased dependence on caregivers, more limited ability to communicate or report abuse, and cognitive and processing difficulties that increase vulnerability to manipulation and reduce children's ability to judge risk. Finally, youth with disabilities are often more likely to exhibit behavior problems, which may result in behaviors that provoke anger and frustration in both adults and peers.

Gay, Lesbian, Bisexual, or Transgender Youth

Sexual minorities—youth who identify as lesbian, gay, bisexual, transgender, or who appear gender nonconforming with respect to appearance and behavior—are also at increased risk for experiencing traumatic incidents. This is primarily due to increases in victimization, including child physical abuse, sexual abuse, emotional abuse, neglect, and bullying (Kosciw, 2004; Roberts, Rosario, Corliss, Koenen, & Austin, 2012). Many of these students are not finding support at home: a significant proportion of homeless youth also identify as lesbian, gay, bisexual, or transgender. They report having left home or being thrown out by caregivers who could not accept their sexual orientation or gender preference (Durso & Gates, 2012). Unfortunately, school is also not a safe haven for these youth: 75% of sexual minority students surveyed reported feeling unsafe at school (Kosciw, 2004).

Polyvictimized Youth

Approximately 8% of children in the United States have been identified as having experienced multiple types of trauma, with particularly high risk for serious negative outcomes (Finkelhor, Turner, Hamby, & Ormrod, 2011). These polyvictimized youth face seemingly insurmountable circumstances: They are more likely to have experienced serious or life-threatening victimization, are more likely to experience victimization in the context of other stressful life circumstances, are more likely to experience serious psychological and behavioral symptoms, and their victimization is likely to persist over time (Finkelhor et al., 2011). The chaotic and stressful situations in which these students are living make it even less likely that they will receive needed intervention. Identification of these vulnerable students and intervention by caring and informed school personnel becomes their best chance for interruption of the cycle of trauma in their lives.

CONCLUSION

Rates of victimization and trauma exposure among children indicate that this experience is very common. Thus, school mental health providers should consider trauma exposure when working with students. Approaches that screen all students who are struggling at school, with particular attention paid to youth who are members of particularly vulnerable groups (e.g., sexual and ethnic minorities, immigrants, youth growing up in poverty, and youth with disabilities), can help detect those students who are "flying under the radar," so they do not continue to suffer in silence.

2

Impact of Trauma Exposure on Children

In the previous chapter, we learned that trauma exposure is common among children and adolescents. Some of the scars left behind by trauma are visible, but most are not. Although humans respond to extreme stress in broadly similar ways, trauma is a singularly individual and subjective experience. Therefore, current definitions of trauma go beyond the event to focus on the individual's experience of the event as well as the long-lasting effects of this experience. The Substance Abuse and Mental Health Services Administration (2014) provides the following definition of *trauma* (sometimes referred to as the three Es):

> Individual trauma results from an *event*, series of events, or set of circumstances that is *experienced* by an individual as physically or emotionally harmful or life threatening and that has lasting adverse *effects* on the individual's functioning and mental, physical, social, emotional, or spiritual well-being. (p. 1)

http://dx.doi.org/10.1037/0000072-003
Creating Healing School Communities: School-Based Interventions for Students Exposed to Trauma, by C. D. Santiago, T. Raviv, and L. H. Jaycox
Copyright © 2018 by the American Psychological Association. All rights reserved.

While many students prove resilient over time, other young victims of trauma suffer in silence, due to shame, fear, difficulty putting their experiences into words, and stigma. The negative impact of trauma can range from the development of posttraumatic stress disorder (PTSD), anxiety, or depression to poor school functioning, decreased rates of high school graduation, and aggressive and delinquent behavior (Costello, Erkanli, Fairbank, & Angold, 2002; Lynch, 2003; Overstreet & Mathews, 2011). In this chapter, we provide an overview of the common negative outcomes resulting from trauma exposure, including effects on learning and school performance, which are particularly relevant for schools. We also discuss how trauma may disrupt healthy development among school-age children and adolescents.

TRAUMA, MENTAL HEALTH, AND BEHAVIOR

Whereas many children may return to previous levels of functioning following a traumatic event, the development of PTSD, depression, anxiety, and behavioral problems is common. For example, one study suggests that children exposed to trauma have nearly double the rates of mental health disorders compared with those without trauma exposure (Copeland, Keeler, Angold, & Costello, 2007). The prevalence of PTSD and other common disorders following traumatic exposure varies among children across studies. In a representative national survey, prevalence estimates by gender were 3.7% for males and 6.3% for females for PTSD and 7.4% for males and 13.9% for females for major depressive disorder (Kilpatrick et al., 2003). In an earlier survey among urban adolescents in Detroit, lifetime prevalence of PTSD was 10.4% for females and 6% for their male counterparts (Breslau, Davis, Andreski, & Peterson, 1991). These are rates for diagnosis of PTSD, but subthreshold levels of PTSD symptoms are more common and often impede functioning. For example, rates of symptoms can be even higher after disasters or large-scale events that affect the functioning of an entire community—11.6% of students in Grades 4–12 in New York City reported PTSD symptoms 6 months after the terrorist attacks of September 11 (Hoven et al., 2005), whereas 55% of students reported moderate to severe symptoms of PTSD after hurricane Andrew in Florida (Vernberg, La Greca, Silverman, & Prinstein, 1996). Even though rates vary, it is important for school mental health providers to support all students in the immediate aftermath of exposure to trauma and to be aware that some students may experience longer lasting difficulties requiring additional support and intervention.

Reactions to trauma can also vary by developmental level, with very young students expressing distress differently than middle and high school students. The National Child Traumatic Stress Network (NCTSN) developed *Child Trauma Toolkit for Educators* (2008) that describes these differences and provides guidance to educators on what they may observe in students exposed to trauma. Across ages, many students will display anxiety, fear, and worry. Young children may appear more irritable or whiny, reverting to more childlike behaviors. Older students may withdraw, have difficulties with attention and concentration, or engage in substance use.

Students who experience trauma may respond by being on guard for additional danger, an understandable response but one that over time could interfere with functioning. In children and adolescents, reactions to trauma may be consistent with PTSD, anxiety, depression, or a combination of these. As discussed in Chapter 1, some students experience multiple traumas and adversities. As these incidents of victimization accumulate, the impact on mental health is intensified. Among students who have experienced multiple traumas (e.g., family violence, child maltreatment, sexual assault, community or school violence), we are more likely to see higher levels of depression and related symptoms (Turner, Finkelhor, & Ormrod, 2006). Cumulative trauma may also be associated with a complex symptom set, which includes both PTSD symptoms and a disruption in interpersonal and affective regulation abilities (Cloitre et al., 2009).

Symptoms of PTSD include repetitive and intrusive thoughts related to the trauma; avoidance of situations, people, or places that are associated with the trauma; hypervigilance; difficulties with attention and concentration; and reexperiencing the event (American Psychiatric Association, 2013). In the classroom, teachers may notice that the student is frequently fatigued or sleepy (because of difficulty sleeping at night), becomes easily startled, seems on edge, is resistant to certain activities that may be related in obvious or not obvious ways to the trauma that was experienced, or has frequent complaints of physical ailments such as stomachaches or headaches. Depression symptoms include low mood, sadness, sleep disturbance, irritability, hopelessness, and thoughts of death or dying (American Psychiatric Association, 2013). Teachers may notice that students appear withdrawn or fatigued in class or may display low motivation and lack of interest in school or extracurricular activities. Anxiety symptoms include worry, avoidance behaviors, somatic complaints, and difficulty concentrating (American Psychiatric Association, 2013). Educators and school mental health providers may notice nervousness or frequent trips to the nurse's office for physical complaints (e.g., stomachaches) as well as avoidance. The case of William describes a student with PTSD symptoms as well as early signs of depression following a trauma.

Eight-year-old William witnessed the car accident resulting in the death of his sister, as described in Chapter 1. After this traumatic loss, William began exhibiting increased worry and fear for his own safety and that of his family members. He frequently complains of stomachaches and has difficulty sleeping. When he is able to sleep, he often experiences dreams about the accident and wakes up distressed. Although William had previously walked to school with his mother, he is now refusing to go. His father is able to convince him to attend school when he drives him the short distance to school, but William is not able to walk home independently. In addition, William appears more withdrawn than before the accident and appears less interested in activities that used to excite him, like playing soccer and video games. He cries frequently and is often irritable. William's symptoms of anxiety, fear, avoidance, and sleep disturbance are common PTSD reactions. His other symptoms (withdrawal, less interest in previously enjoyable activities, sadness, irritability) are related to loss and grief. However, if they continue or intensify, they may indicate a depressive disorder.

Educators and school mental health providers may also notice behavioral problems or aggression following trauma. Not surprisingly, children exposed to family violence often exhibit verbally or physically aggressive behaviors (Chan & Yeung, 2009). Similarly, students who experience violence at school, such as witnessing someone being threatened, hit, or beaten up, are more likely to show violent behavior themselves along with PTSD reactions (Flannery, Wester, & Singer, 2004). Exposure to violence in the neighborhood or community is also linked with aggressive behavior, especially for boys (Flannery et al., 2004; Mohammad, Shapiro, Wainwright, & Carter, 2015). Similar to internalizing symptoms, anger and aggression continue to intensify among students who have experienced multiple traumas (Turner et al., 2006). Thus, students who witness or who are victims of violence may act out and engage in similar violent behavior. These students may need trauma-related treatment in order to adaptively manage their reactions and behavior. The case of Kenneth describes a student with externalizing symptoms following a history of multiple traumas.

As described in Chapter 1, twelve-year-old Kenneth has experienced domestic violence, physical abuse, unstable housing, and community violence. Although Kenneth displays a number of internalizing symptoms, his behavioral symptoms are more often noticed by his mother and teachers. Kenneth's mother reports that he often refuses to help with chores and appears angry and irritable with her at home. When asked a question in class or to do in-class work, Kenneth often refuses or responds with an angry outburst. Because of this, he is often asked to leave class. Most recently, he pushed over a desk when leaving class, and school administrators are discussing whether to suspend him. The school counselor, who has a positive relationship with Kenneth, is concerned that he is depressed, which influences his irritability and motivation in school. She is worried that suspension will only increase his hopelessness about his future. Kenneth's presentation is not uncommon after a history of multiple traumas. His risk for suspension and possibly dropping out of school is high.

THE EFFECT OF TRAUMA ON LEARNING AND SCHOOL PERFORMANCE

Educators and school mental health providers may notice an immediate impact on student academics following a trauma, but sometimes the difficulties take time to become apparent. After experiencing trauma, students may be less engaged in school or perform more poorly on homework and tests (Bethell, Newacheck, Hawes, & Halfon, 2014; Sharkey, 2010). Even learning about the occurrence of a recent local homicide, regardless of whether the victim was known to the student, affects how students perform on vocabulary and reading assessments (Sharkey, 2010). In the long term, trauma may affect student IQ, reading ability, and the likelihood of needing to repeat grades (Bethell et al., 2014; Delaney-Black et al., 2002; Porche, Costello, & Rosen-Reynoso, 2016). PTSD symptoms, including not being able to stop thinking about seeing something scary, difficulty sleeping, and worrying about people being shot while in class, also interfere with children's ability to read (Delaney-Black et al., 2002), which can have long-term implications for school performance. In fact, family trauma has been linked to increased risk for repeating a grade, being on an individualized education program, and poor school engagement through child mental health problems (Porche et al., 2016).

Children who experience many traumas may have more pronounced difficulties with learning and academic performance (Perfect, Turley, Carlson, Yohanna, & Pfenninger Saint Gilles, 2016). Those with repeated exposure may have difficulty with basic attention, memory, and problem-solving skills. For example, children exposed to familial trauma (e.g., domestic violence, abuse) showed weaker skills in attention, memory, and processing speed compared with those not exposed to trauma (DePrince, Weinzierl, & Combs, 2009). These deficits impact day-to-day learning and ultimately long-term academic achievement and IQ. Among a sample of adolescents exposed to multiple traumas, trauma stemming from abuse was related to lower IQ; the PTSD-related symptoms of reexperiencing and arousal explain this link (Kira, Lewandowski, Somers, Yoon, & Chiodo,

2012). Dissociative symptoms (memory problems, unresponsiveness, flashbacks) among trauma-exposed youth also interfere with feelings of school belonging, academic competence, and performance on standardized achievement tests (Perzow et al., 2013). Thus, after experiencing trauma, students may feel as though the event is happening again or they may feel on edge and irritable, all of which make it difficult to pay attention, to concentrate, and to take on new information or skills. These difficulties are illustrated in Sydnee's case. Sydnee's lack of attention and her confusion may be due to reexperiencing (feeling like the hurricane is happening again), rumination (thinking about the hurricane even when she doesn't want to), or emotional numbing. Sydnee's sleep problems are likely to exacerbate the effects of the trauma. A sense of foreshortened future and general irritability may explain why Sydnee is sometime frustrated and hopeless about school.

Fifteen-year-old Sydnee lived through a Category 4 hurricane, as described in Chapter 1. After the hurricane, Sydnee began displaying symptoms of PTSD, including worry about the safety of her family members, feeling like the hurricane was happening again, difficulty sleeping, a sense of a foreshortened future, and difficulty concentrating. These symptoms are interfering with her school performance. Prior to the hurricane, Sydnee achieved mostly As and Bs and worked hard in school. Although she had a lot of family responsibility outside of school, she managed to stay on track with assignments and generally enjoyed school. Recently, her teachers have noticed that she doesn't seem to be paying attention in class and sometimes appears confused when she is called on. One teacher in particular noted that Sydnee is behind on several assignments. When asked about it, Sydnee sometimes appears concerned that her schoolwork is suffering and says she is trying to catch up. However, at other times, Sydnee responds with frustration and defiance, asking, "What's the point?"

TRAUMA AND PHYSICAL HEALTH

Some students who have experienced trauma may visit the nurse's office frequently or miss school due to illness. Trauma affects not only children's emotional and behavioral functioning but also their physical health. Research suggests that trauma can alter neurobiological stress systems, which can impact children's developing bodies and brains over time (Gunnar & Quevedo, 2007). For example, trauma exposure can alter the body's regulatory processes as children develop; the subsequent elevated levels of stress hormones may negatively affect brain maturation (see De Bellis & Zisk, 2014, for a review). Furthermore, evidence suggests that children who have experienced several violence-related traumas (e.g., bullying, witnessing domestic violence, physical abuse) have shorter *telomeres*, repetitive sequences at the end of linear chromosomes that can be understood as a marker of premature cellular aging (Shalev et al., 2013).

Researchers suggest that the alterations in the body's biological stress response systems in turn influence the development of both mental health problems (e.g., PTSD, depression, behavior problems) and physical disease (e.g., cardiovascular disease, obesity, gastrointestinal disorders, chronic pain; De Bellis & Zisk, 2014). Indeed, children exposed to trauma are more likely to have chronic health conditions, such as asthma or obesity (Bethell et al., 2014). Furthermore, children who experience PTSD symptoms following a trauma are at even higher risk for health problems, including asthma and gastrointestinal problems (Graham-Bermann & Seng, 2005). In the groundbreaking Adverse Childhood Experiences Study (Felitti et al., 1998), traumatic childhood experiences such as abuse and domestic violence as well as other stressful exposures were examined in relationship to adult health. The number of adverse childhood exposures showed a graded relationship to the presence of adult diseases including heart disease, cancer, chronic lung disease, skeletal fractures, and liver disease (Felitti et al., 1998). Although many of these effects develop over time, it is important for educators and school mental health providers to be aware that somatic complaints and illness could be linked to traumatic stress. Furthermore, facilitating treatment for children exposed to trauma and displaying distress may help prevent some of these long-term consequences.

DISRUPTIONS TO HEALTHY DEVELOPMENT

Taking a developmental framework when working with children and adolescents exposed to trauma is essential. In school, children are working on meeting major developmental milestones and learning key academic skills. Elementary students are tasked with developing academic and social skills as they have increased interaction with peers in the classroom and are expected to be developing increased self-control and emotion regulation (Holmbeck, Devine, & Bruno, 2010). Adolescents begin to develop higher order cognitive skills and face increasing academic demands, while also experiencing pubertal development and developing a sense of autonomy and identity (Holmbeck et al., 2010). While it is typical to have stress and challenges as children navigate these milestones, trauma and related psychological symptoms can impede children's development.

As discussed above, trauma can lead to PTSD, anxiety, depression, and behavioral problems (Copeland et al., 2007). Trauma can also negatively affect academic performance (Bethell et al., 2014) and disrupt biological regulatory systems (De Bellis & Zisk, 2014). Symptoms of PTSD, anxiety, or depression may prevent young elementary students from developing positive peer relationships and seriously disrupt students' ability to adaptively regulate emotions. Difficulty concentrating may further impact academic skills. Adolescents exposed to trauma may struggle to balance increasing demands at school and master higher order cognitive skills. Peer relationships and identity development may also suffer if adolescents are struggling with significant symptoms following trauma. Furthermore, trauma can negatively affect the developing brain, interfering with networks linked to regulating thought processes, motivations, behaviors, and a sense of self (De Bellis & Zisk, 2014). These regulatory processes are essential for healthy social and emotional and academic development. Thus, our goal as we work with children and adolescents is not only to reduce symptoms and distress but to support them in being able to reach and navigate major developmental milestones.

CONCLUSION

Trauma exposure among children is linked to PTSD, anxiety, depression, poor school functioning, decreased rates of high school graduation, and aggressive and delinquent behavior (Costello et al., 2002; Lynch, 2003; Overstreet & Mathews, 2011). In school, children may present with anxiety or fear, distrust, somatic complaints, avoidance behaviors, and/or display changes in behavior (NCTSN, 2008). These types of symptoms interfere with school engagement and academic skill development (Bethell et al., 2014; Delaney-Black et al., 2002). The case vignettes (William, Kenneth, and Sydnee) remind us that although there are commonalities in reactions to trauma, children and adolescents can also present differently, and these reactions can significantly influence daily functioning and long-term development.

This chapter summarized the ways that trauma can disrupt functioning, but there are many reasons to remain hopeful. Many children are resilient and return to previous levels of functioning following trauma. In addition, research suggests that some youth experience posttraumatic growth, or positive change stemming from coping with trauma, and that supportive adults can facilitate this growth (Kilmer et al., 2014). For students who are in need of intervention to support healthy functioning, schools may be an ideal setting to deliver such support, and this is the focus of the next chapter.

3

The Rationale
for School-Based Interventions

Many school mental health providers are keenly aware of the need for trauma-focused interventions in schools, and indeed, scientific evidence shows that such programs are imperative in order to meet the needs of the most vulnerable and underserved students (Jaycox, Stein, & Amaya-Jackson, 2008). Many students are affected by trauma, particularly in urban schools (see Chapter 1, this volume), and trauma exposure has a clearly detrimental impact on learning, which is the primary mission of schools (Chapter 2). Unfortunately, those most likely to be exposed to trauma are also the most likely to go without any formal mental health care; bringing such services into schools overcomes many of the barriers faced by the nation's most vulnerable youth. The U.S. Surgeon General's National Action Agenda for Children's Mental Health and the President's New Freedom Commission both recommend social–emotional support in schools to improve access to care for all students (Olin & Hoagwood, 2002; U.S.

http://dx.doi.org/10.1037/0000072-004
Creating Healing School Communities: School-Based Interventions for Students Exposed to Trauma,
by C. D. Santiago, T. Raviv, and L. H. Jaycox
Copyright © 2018 by the American Psychological Association. All rights reserved.

Department of Health and Human Services, 2003). As we describe in this chapter, trauma-focused interventions are highly compatible with existing school mental health models and can therefore meet this urgent need.

BARRIERS TO ACCESSING MENTAL HEALTH SERVICES

On average, only 25% of children with mental health needs receive services. Of those children who do receive mental health services, 70% to 80% receive those services in schools (The Center for Health and Healthcare in Schools, 2012). Children with trauma exposure may be even more likely to go without needed care. Low-income minority children are at increased risk for violence exposure and mental health problems because of multiple risk factors, including poverty (Coulton et al., 1995; Garbarino, 1995; Straussner & Straussner, 1997) and school and community factors (Oswald et al., 1999). However, these children are less likely to receive traditional mental health services (Garrison, Roy, & Azar, 1999; U.S. Public Health Service, 2000). In addition, it is known that traumatized individuals have lower odds of seeking health services than their nontraumatized counterparts (Guterman, Hahm, & Cameron, 2002). The natural desire to want to avoid thinking or talking about a traumatic event can keep some from seeking care. There are many possible reasons for unmet mental health care needs among children. The lack of universal screening measures means that sometimes the problem is not detected at all. Once identified, many families face difficulty accessing convenient and affordable care, while stigma and lack of trust can also deter families from seeking help. Exhibit 3.1 lists some of the most common barriers to receipt of mental health care for children (McKay & Bannon, 2004; Owens et al., 2002).

ADVANTAGES TO SCHOOL-BASED SERVICES

Delivering mental health services through the school system can address these structural barriers that often prevent students from receiving needed services (Garrison et al., 1999). For example, school-based services eliminate many burdens on families related to transportation, time, cost, and availability.

Exhibit 3.1

Common Barriers to Seeking Mental Health Care for Children

- Perception of mental health
  - Problem isn't serious enough
  - Can handle problem on own
- Perception of services
  - Low trust in person who recommended help
  - Trusted individuals do not recommend getting help
  - Lack of confidence that services will help
  - Prior negative experience
  - Stigma (concern over what family and friends would say)
  - Child does not want to go
- Structural barriers
  - Failure to detect the problem
  - Too expensive
  - Inconvenient
  - Distance and transportation
  - Difficulty locating services
  - Waiting lists (too few qualified providers)

In addition to circumventing structural barriers, school-based services can address many of the perceptual barriers by having trusted, known school personnel engage the family in a familiar, nonstigmatizing setting. Thus, schools have been identified as an ideal entry point for improving access to mental health services for children (Allensworth et al., 1997). In fact, studies have documented that the most common source of mental health services for students who need them is provided through schools (Farmer, Stangl, Burns, Costello, & Angold, 1999), usually by a school counselor.

A recent example related to trauma interventions for students who lived through the hurricanes in New Orleans highlights the potential for schools to increase accessibility for treatment. Project Fleur de Lis conducted a study in which students were screened and selected for intervention and then randomized to receive either a school group-based intervention or a dyadic (parent–child) intervention based at a family clinic within 10 miles of the schools (Jaycox et al., 2010). In the school-based intervention, 98% of students started the groups and 91% finished them. In contrast, in the clinic-based intervention, 37% started the intervention, 23% continued after some students were excluded for insufficient symptoms, and only 9% completed treatment, even after participants were offered reimbursement for transportation, free babysitting at the clinic, and flexible appointment times. Students improved in both types of treatment, but many more were served successfully in the school setting than in the clinic setting.

In circumstances such as New Orleans after the hurricane, schools are sometimes thrust into the position of addressing trauma as a result of a communitywide or schoolwide disaster or tragedy. In such cases, schools serve as a stabilizing environment and thus play a role in facilitating recovery following mass tragedy and disaster (Amaya-Jackson et al., 2003; Macy, 2003; National Child Traumatic Stress Network, National Center for PTSD, 2006). But work in this area to date has shown both researchers and clinicians that focusing on the particular crisis is not enough. For example, following Hurricanes Katrina and Rita in New Orleans, students reported many other traumatic experiences, such as family and community violence, sudden deaths, and accidents, and total trauma exposure was the best predictor of current distress (Langley, Cohen, et al., 2013). Thus, efforts to address a crisis or disaster often are dual-use and allow schools to build capacity to address problems among children exposed to other types of traumatic events at other points in time.

Children spend an average of 35 hours per week in their school building, surrounded by adults with knowledge of their academic and social functioning. This knowledge and access translates into our best opportunity to detect problems early and improve access to interventions that can support student success and potentially prevent the need for more intensive, specialized, and expensive mental health interventions. Furthermore, schools are mandated to educate all children. When students' academic and social functioning is negatively affected by their emotional or behavioral difficulties, and they lack the ability to access mental health services outside of schools, the ability of schools to meet their educational needs often means addressing their unmet mental health care needs. However, despite the promise of schools as a venue for reaching underserved children with trauma-related mental health problems, there is still a substantial gap between educational and mental health policies (Kataoka, Rowan, & Hoagwood, 2009). In the section that follows, we discuss the two major ways that this gap is being bridged.

NATIONAL EFFORTS TO IMPROVE CHILD MENTAL HEALTH IN SCHOOLS

Two strands of work support the concept that a supportive, trauma-informed school is more successful in its educational mission. The first is the movement to incorporate social–emotional learning (SEL) into school curricula and learning standards, and the second is to support students through a multitiered system of intervention so that they can receive the appropriate level of support to be successful. School mental health providers often support educators in implementing SEL programs as well as provide interventions themselves within a multitiered system.

Social–Emotional Learning

Educators have long recognized the need to address SEL alongside reading and math. The Collaborative for Academic, Social, and Emotional Learning (CASEL) was founded in 1994 and published its first of several guides, "Promoting Social and Emotional Learning: Guidelines for Educators," in 1997. Five core competencies are identified: being self-aware, being able to regulate emotions, being socially aware, having good relationship skills, and demonstrating responsible decision-making (see Exhibit 3.2; Weissberg & Cascarino, 2013). A recent analysis of over 200 studies of SEL programming in schools concluded that SEL programs implemented by educators not only improved social skills, behavior, and emotional functioning but also promoted more positive attitudes toward school and were linked to gains in academic achievement (Durlak, Weissberg, Dymnicki, Taylor, & Schellinger, 2011). Thus, there is strong scientific evidence that

---

Exhibit 3.2

Five Core Competencies of Social–Emotional Learning

1. Self-Awareness
2. Ability to Regulate Emotions
3. Social Awareness
4. Good Relationship Skills
5. Responsible Decision-Making

SEL programs can promote mental health while also strengthening the school's core mission of education.

With the recent advent of the Common Core State Standards in 2010 (National Governors Association Center for Best Practices, Council of Chief State School Officers, 2010), many were concerned about the standards' focus on English and math and lack of emphasis on SEL. In fact, as the 45 states that adopted the Common Core struggle with implementation, they are finding ways to retain a focus on SEL concepts. For instance, one common core math standard is students "make sense of problems and persevere in solving them," and according to Zakrzewski (2014), this concept draws on SEL skills of self-efficacy, attention control, managing stress, regulating emotions, and more. CASEL (2016) is advocating for SEL experts to be engaged in the implementation plans for the Common Core, so as to find ways to integrate SEL into the academic learning. Elias (2014) pointed out that the Common Core standards require students to be able to elaborate their reasoning, exhibit strategic thinking, persevere in the face of difficulty, be oriented toward independence, and possess social and emotional competencies in order to achieve the college and career readiness goals.

A few states, such as Kansas, Pennsylvania, and Illinois, have incorporated SEL recommendations into their learning standards. For instance, the State of Illinois was the first state to develop its own learning standards related to SEL. The Illinois's Children's Mental Health Act of 2003 called for a plan for the Board of Education to incorporate such standards "for the purpose of enhancing and measuring children's school readiness and ability to achieve academic success" (Section 15(a), Public Act 93-0495). For

Illinois, the three goals are to "develop self-awareness and self-management skills to achieve school life and success, use self-awareness and interpersonal skills to establish and maintain positive relationships, and demonstrate decision-making skills and responsible behaviors in personal, school, and community contexts" (Illinois State Board of Education, 2016).

These efforts to incorporate SEL into curricula and learning standards are directly in line with efforts to develop trauma-informed programming, as we discuss in Chapters 4, 5, and 6. When educators understand the ways that trauma exposure can disrupt the development of emotion regulation, conflict resolution, and social relationships, they are better equipped to address these challenges among their students and support them in progress toward these goals. Furthermore, many of the learning standards are compatible with the common, core elements of trauma-focused interventions, and participation in these interventions can help students exposed to trauma develop the skills they need to succeed in school and beyond.

Multi-Tiered Systems of Supports

Another strand of work in schools relates to models that ensure adequate supports for students in need. This field is evolving, with two earlier models more recently merged to create the Multi-Tiered Systems of Supports (MTSS) model. The first model, called Response to Intervention (RTI), was designed to identify students with academic struggles early and implement needed evidence-based academic interventions to ensure their success. RTI was introduced with the reauthorization of the Individuals With Disabilities Education Improvement Act (IDEIA) of 2004 (Fletcher & Vaughan, 2009). A parallel model, called Positive Behavior Intervention and Supports (PBIS), was similar to RTI but addressed students with behavioral rather than academic difficulties and was recommended by IDEIA (2004) as a way to ensure a safe learning environment. Both models incorporated different tiers of intervention, an evidence-based approach, and the use of data to determine success or the need for adjustments (Jimerson, Burns, & VanDerHeyden, 2007). More recently, however, these two models have been combined into a more comprehensive model, MTSS, which addresses both academics and behavior. Currently MTSS models have been developed and are being implemented by many school districts. These models tend to take a more systemic approach to consider both individual learners along with a "whole school, prevention-based" approach that uses a "layered continuum of evidence based practices and systems" (Colorado Department of Education, 2016). The MTSS framework is illustrated in Figure 3.1.

The key aspect of all three of these models draws from public health models that describe tiered interventions: a universal approach for all students (Tier 1), a targeted approach for those with elevated risk or indication of need (Tier 2), and a more intensive approach reserved for the few in the greatest need (Tier 3). The MTSS model, however, adds in more systemwide aspects of overall school improvement, professional development, and supports for instruction. These aspects are particularly relevant to efforts to create "trauma-sensitive schools," in which all educators and support staff are equipped with the training and support they need to work together to create a safe and supportive climate for all students, regardless of whether they have been exposed to trauma. School mental health providers are essential to interventions across tiers. They may be involved in trauma-focused professional development for educators and in providing trauma interventions directly to students. We discuss universal approaches further in Chapter 4 and targeted and intensive interventions for trauma in Chapter 7.

CONCLUSION

Children spend a substantial portion of their time in schools. Schools have the potential to reduce barriers to accessing treatment and serve as a non-stigmatizing entry point for treatment. By addressing students' mental health needs, schools are better able to support their educational development and learning. Both the SEL movement and the MTSS model provide excellent frameworks for understanding the various aspects of trauma-related interventions available to schools. Interventions at various tiers can improve social-emotional functioning as well as academic performance, absences, and behavior. We use the MTSS framework in Chapters 4 and 6 to categorize and describe the possible interventions and their evidence to date.

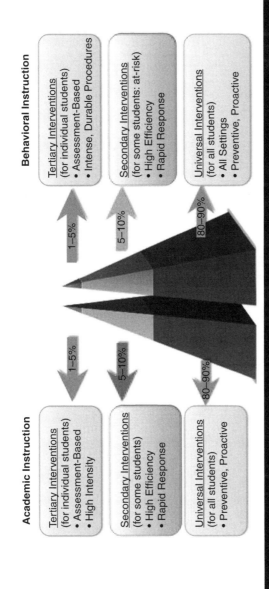

Figure 3.1

Designing schoolwide systems for student success. From *Multi-Tiered System of Support (MTSS) & PBIS*, by the Office of Special Education Programs Technical Assistance Center for Positive Behavioral Interventions and Support, 2016. Retrieved from http://www.pbis.org/school/mtss. Copyright 2016 by the Office of Special Education Programs Technical Assistance Center for Positive Behavioral Interventions and Support. Reprinted with permission.

4

Universal and Schoolwide Interventions for Trauma

Chapter 3 described the Multi-Tiered System of Supports (MTSS) framework; here we focus on Tier I of this model: universal schoolwide policies, practices, and interventions to support students exposed to trauma. In all schools, structure, rules, and positive climate are crucial to support students' ability to learn and perform. In schools with a high proportion of students affected by trauma, and in schools that are located in communities characterized by poverty, violence, and unpredictability, creating schools that are safe havens and where positive behavior is encouraged and rewarded becomes even more essential. In schools without this foundation, school mental health providers quickly become overwhelmed with requests to support students whose behaviors are interfering with learning, students who are subjected to bullying or other victimization, or students who are disengaged or not attending school. Therefore, we strongly recommend that efforts to support recovery from

http://dx.doi.org/10.1037/0000072-005
Creating Healing School Communities: School-Based Interventions for Students Exposed to Trauma,
by C. D. Santiago, T. Raviv, and L. H. Jaycox
Copyright © 2018 by the American Psychological Association. All rights reserved.

trauma among students begin with an overarching plan to embed supports within a trauma-informed climate. Before turning to this discussion, we briefly review two helpful frameworks that provide guidance on the creation of trauma-informed schools: the concept of trauma and the trauma-informed approach advocated by Substance Abuse and Mental Health Services Administration (SAMHSA; 2014) and the Trauma and Learning Policy Initiative's Flexible Framework (Cole, Eisner, Gregory, & Ristuccia, 2013).

As the widespread and damaging effects of exposure to trauma have become increasingly well understood, the need for a broad public health approach to mitigate its emotional and financial costs has been recognized. In response, SAMHSA published *Concept of Trauma and Guidance for a Trauma-Informed Approach* in 2014. The SAMHSA approach is specifically designed to be applicable to different systems, including not only education but also other child-serving systems such as child welfare and juvenile justice. This broad framework is articulated in a set of four assumptions.

> A program, organization, or system that is trauma-informed *realizes* the widespread impact of trauma and understands potential paths for recovery; *recognizes* the signs and symptoms of trauma in clients, families, staff, and others involved with the system; and *responds* by fully integrating knowledge about trauma into policies, procedures, and practices, and seeks to actively *resist re-traumatization*. (Substance Abuse and Mental Health Services Administration, 2014, p. 9; italics in original)

The SAMHSA framework is further articulated by six principles, which include ensuring safety, creating a culture of trustworthiness in which there are opportunities for collaboration, peer support, and empowerment of all stakeholders, with attention to culturally sensitive practices. The SAMHSA approach also clearly states that implementation of a trauma-informed approach must occur within various domains, beginning with governance and leadership, extending to training and workforce development, and encompassing the physical environment, among others. Although intuitively appealing, generated by groups of experts in the field, and extensively vetted, the SAMHSA model is still new, and no research to date has been conducted to explore factors related to implementation, adoption, or resulting improvements in the functioning of agencies.

The Trauma and Learning Policy Initiative vision for a trauma-sensitive school shares much with the SAMHSA framework. In particular, their vision includes the following six attributes:

1. Leadership and staff share an understanding of how trauma impacts learning and why a schoolwide approach is needed.
2. The school supports all students to feel physically, socially, emotional, and academically safe.
3. The school addresses students' needs in holistic ways, taking into account their relationships, self-regulation, academic competence, and physical and emotional well-being.
4. The school explicitly connects students to the school community.
5. The school embraces teamwork and a sense of shared responsibility for all students.
6. Leadership and staff anticipate and adapt to the ever-changing needs of students and the community. (Cole et al., 2013, pp. 18–25)

Like the SAMHSA model, the Trauma and Learning Policy Initiative vision emphasizes the importance of a systemwide ("whole-school") approach that emphasizes knowledge about trauma among all members of the community, the importance of creating an environment that is physically and emotionally safe, supporting relationships and students' self-regulatory skills, and the importance of collaboration and shared responsibility. Likewise, initiative materials also explicitly articulate domains of implementation that should be included in a comprehensive action plan, including leadership, professional development, academic and nonacademic strategies that enhance learning, access to resources and services, and collaboration with families. The Trauma and Learning Policy Initiative approach emphasizes the role that educators, not mental health providers, play in creating a safe and supportive climate for all students. That being said, the role of a school mental health provider is critical. Specific tasks that are well suited to the knowledge and skills of school mental health providers include serving on steering committees or work groups charged with leading the work of planning and implementing steps that will contribute to becoming a trauma-informed school, providing professional development, continuing education, and technical assistance to educators and others about the impact of trauma on students, consulting with teachers on how best to support specific students impacted by trauma within the classroom setting, and serving as a resource for helping to identify and serve students who may need more specialized behavioral health interventions. Specific steps for the Trauma and Learning Policy Initiative approach are described on the website (https://traumasensitiveschools.org/; see Resource #2 in the Resources section at the end of this book). As with the SAMHSA model, although descriptive examples and case studies of individual schools' implementation of trauma-sensitive practices have been publicized, to date practitioners have not rigorously studied the implementation or effectiveness of these types of efforts. Next, we review some universal approaches to supporting students exposed to trauma.

SCHOOL CULTURE, CLIMATE, AND CONNECTEDNESS

By its nature, the experience of trauma threatens perceptions of safety, can impair the formation and maintenance of healthy relationships, and heightens sensitivity to threat. Humans are social creatures, and learning occurs in a social context, which underscores the importance of creating a culture that emphasizes safety and the establishment of positive relationships. We return to our case vignettes to share student perspectives on their school experiences. Although these students are in need of more intensive interventions (described in Chapters 6 and 7), they still benefit from universal approaches that emphasize safety and positive relationships.

Schoolwide Positive Behavioral Interventions and Support

In its definition of *positive school climate*, the National School Climate Council includes "norms, values, and expectations that support people feeling socially, emotionally, and physically safe" and in which students, educators, and families work together (Thapa, Cohen, Guffey, & Higgins-D'Alessandro, 2013, p. 2). School climate has been associated with a variety

When asked about his relationship with school, 12-year-old Kenneth states, "In this school, you can't let people think you're a punk or you're gonna get jumped after school. So I can't let people disrespect me. That's why I keep getting suspended, but the principal doesn't care about that. I don't talk to my teachers about our family business—they wouldn't understand anyway. They're always just on my case about something. They always focus on the things that don't really matter, like if I'm wearing a hat in their class. But they don't even notice or ask what is going on, like if I come in late because gang bangers were hassling me on the street, they're just like, 'you're late again' and send me to the office. I had only one teacher, in fifth grade, who really cared. He would just ask a little bit, like 'hey, you cool?' when he saw me in the hallway. He let me come sit in his room during lunch if I was having a bad day. But that was at my old school. There's no point trying to talk to teachers here. I probably won't even be going to this school next year."

In conversations about her academic performance, Sydnee states, "Sometimes it's just too much. I feel like I can't even make it through the day, and here is this teacher asking me to memorize vocabulary words in Spanish. Sometimes I just feel invisible in school. I mean, I used to be an A–B student at my old school, before the hurricane. Now I'm barely passing some of my classes. It feels like my teachers think I should be over it by now, but they don't understand that what I saw, what I lived through—I can't just put it behind me. The teachers that get it, you know, the ones who say, 'I know you're having a hard time right now, how can I help you make a plan to make up the work?', the ones that make time to talk about real things and not just school things, those are the teachers that make me want to keep going. But other teachers are always just, 'you missed this and that' or 'you're gonna have to go to summer school if you don't get down to business' and sometimes I feel like it's hopeless."

of student outcomes, ranging from self-esteem and emotional and mental health outcomes, to risky behavior such as substance use, to academic outcomes including attendance, behavior at school, and academic achievement (Thapa et al., 2013). One approach that emphasizes the implementation of structures that enhance school climate is Schoolwide Positive Behavioral Interventions and Support (SWPBIS). Many schools nationwide are already implementing SWPBIS as a result of research demonstrating that this approach improves perceived safety, academic achievement, student behavior, and social–emotional functioning (Bradshaw, Waasdorp, & Leaf, 2012; Horner et al., 2009; Ward & Gersten, 2013). In brief, the universal portions of SWPBIS implementation involve defining, teaching, and posting schoolwide rules for student behavior, rewarding positive behaviors and compliance with school rules, implementing a consistent and standardized system for responding to violations of rules, and regularly reviewing data to improve implementation and identify problem areas (e.g., hallway, cafeteria) or target groups. As reviewed by Chafouleas, Johnson, Overstreet, and Santos (2016), the SWPBIS model can be easily integrated with models of trauma-informed schools because it emphasizes a whole school approach and the creation of a safe school where positive behaviors are encouraged and rewarded. Thus, many of the universal elements described in this chapter are a good match for the SWPBIS framework. Components that are more specific to trauma-informed practices can be more easily integrated into a school that has already adopted SWPBIS structures and a focus on school climate.

Discipline Practices

Of particular relevance to students affected by trauma is a school's approach to discipline. As reviewed in Chapter 2, students with trauma histories are more likely to exhibit disruptive or aggressive behavior at school, to abuse substances, and to have chronic absenteeism. Unfortunately, without an understanding of the underlying mental health or learning problems that contribute to these behaviors, schools may be more likely to react with discipline practices that emphasize strict consequences, suspensions, or expulsions and unwittingly reinforce these behaviors (Leaf & Keys, 2005) or retraumatize students. Punitive practices that rely on suspensions or even criminalization of relatively minor offenses, such as breaking school rules or failure to appear in court, are ineffective; disproportionately affect minority students and those with disabilities; and increase risk for dropout, truancy, and mental health problems (Morgan, Salomon, Plotkin, & Cohen, 2014). Calls for reform of school discipline practices have been heard from students, parents, educators, and policymakers, prompting the U.S. Departments of Education and Justice to issue new recommendations for improving school climate and reducing exclusionary discipline practices, especially those that disproportionately affect minority students, in 2015. While a comprehensive review of recommendations for discipline reform is beyond the scope of this book, the School Discipline Consensus Report (Morgan et al., 2014) provides several practical recommendations for schools, many of which are consistent with trauma-informed schools as well as SWPBIS.

Professional Development and Education

Integral to efforts to create a trauma-sensitive and supportive school climate is building a shared understanding among all educators and staff interacting with students about how trauma impacts student development, behavior, health, and relationships. Suggested components for trauma awareness training for educators are summarized in Exhibit 4.1 and are described more fully in this section. Often called "Trauma 101," this type of professional development serves several purposes. First and foremost, it aims to shift the perspective on student behavior that can be challenging or puzzling for educators and staff in viewing these behaviors as potentially related to trauma and therefore as opportunities to help, support, or intervene (also known as adopting a "trauma lens"). For example, without an understanding of how trauma is affecting Kenneth and Sydnee, two of the students described in the vignettes, teachers could perceive these students as disrespectful or unmotivated by school. The teacher–student relationship would likely be strained, classroom misbehavior might lead to suspensions, and interventions that would be implemented would be less likely to be successful without addressing the function of the target

---

Exhibit 4.1

Suggested Components for Trauma Awareness Training for Educators

- Definition of trauma, including examples and rates of exposure
- Common classroom and behavioral manifestations of exposure to trauma
- The impact of trauma exposure on brain development and physiology
- Schoolwide strategies for supporting students exposed to trauma
- Classroom strategies for supporting students exposed to trauma
- When and how to refer students who need more intensive mental health support
- Compassion fatigue, secondary traumatic stress, and burnout among adults working with youth affected by trauma and self-care strategies to protect against these negative effects

---

behaviors. Specifically, Kenneth may be responding with aggressive or disruptive behavior when he is reminded of his trauma by an angry adult. Responding with anger and aggression to perceived threats likely has helped Kenneth keep himself physically and emotionally safe in his home or neighborhood. It will take time, practice, and consistent calm responses on the part of his teachers to help Kenneth learn that these responses are not necessary or helpful in the school setting. Often, helping teachers understand that student behaviors are directly related to their experiences outside of the classroom can provide an alternative perspective and alter a teacher's approach to such students.

Part of the Trauma 101 training can focus on increasing understanding of types of trauma encountered by students and rates of exposure (see Chapter 1) and common classroom and behavioral manifestations of exposure to trauma (see Chapter 2). For an audience of educators, a review of the impact of trauma exposure on brain development and physiology can help shed light on the way trauma triggers an activation of the brain's alarm system can disrupt the child's ability to learn. Bruce Perry (2013) and the Child Trauma Academy created a helpful series of brief presentations, the "Seven Slide Series," that explain the impact of trauma on brain development and learning (see Resource #10).

Although receiving basic knowledge about the impact of trauma can in and of itself become an "aha" moment for many educators, building upon an introductory presentation with a more detailed presentation can provide teachers with specific tools to use. Given that educators are not expected to be experts in mental health, clear messages about roles for teachers and staff should be addressed, including a review of mandated reporting standards for suspected abuse or neglect and guidelines on when and how to refer to a school mental health provider. This could also include an emphasis on the importance of routines, strategies for managing transitions, relaxation strategies that can be implemented in the classroom, and relationship building activities, such as morning meetings or advisory time. Providing teachers with tools to recognize trauma triggers and with deescalation strategies that restore safety and calm can help prevent retraumatization. Two examples of this type of approach, from New Haven, Connecticut, and San Francisco, California, are included within a recent *School Mental Health* special issue on trauma-informed schools. D. L. Perry and Daniels (2016) and Dorado, Martinez, McArthur, and Leibovitz (2016) described the processes their programs followed as well as the professional development components of their efforts. In both efforts, results indicated that participating educators and staff reported increased knowledge about trauma and its effects as well as increased use of trauma-sensitive practices. For school mental health professionals interested in providing this type of training, materials are available through several sources. One helpful resource is the National Child Traumatic Stress Network (NCTSN; 2008) *Toolkit for Educators*. Another is *Listen, Protect, Connect—Model & Teach: Psychological First Aid (PFA) for Students and Teachers* (Schreiber, Gurwitch, & Wong, 2006) developed by the Treatment and Services Adaptation Center for Resiliency, Hope, and Wellness in Schools to support educators in promoting healing in students exposed to trauma in schools. See the Resources section of this book for links to these and other key materials.

Teachers, particularly those working in areas with widespread traumatic exposure, should be introduced to the concepts of compassion fatigue and self-care. The term *compassion fatigue* was coined by Charles Figley (1995) and refers to the emotional and physical exhaustion that can result from listening to and supporting individuals coping with trauma and working in environments that may have insufficient resources to meet enormous needs. Compassion fatigue can affect anyone in a helping profession, and it has been linked to emotional symptoms resembling depression or post-traumatic stress, reduced effectiveness at work, and a reduced perception of the value of the work they do. One resource for educators, the NCTSN document *Self Care for Educators*, outlines some warning signs and provides some suggestions on how to combat compassion fatigue.

Relationships Between Educators and Students

While school mental health providers play an important role in providing specialized mental health supports for students coping with trauma (as we review in Chapter 7), school connectedness and a safe and supportive climate are created by coordinated efforts among all educators and staff, from the principal to the office staff, to connect on a personal level and create relationships with all students, especially those who may be more disconnected from adults in their schools and communities. One effective activity that can help reveal students who may require special attention is *relationship mapping*. This activity consists of listing all students in a school, and instructing each adult to place a yellow dot next to the students with whom they feel they have a positive, trusting relationship or whom they believe would approach them with a personal problem, and to place a red dot next to each student they believe to be at risk for academic or personal reasons. Ultimately, this forms a visual of how many supportive relationships each student in the building students has. In our experience, it is not uncommon for the students considered most at-risk (the ones with the most red dots) to have the fewest supportive relationships (yellow dots). Detailed instructions on this activity, including discussion questions and action steps (e.g., assigning staff to mentor those students who have no yellow dots), are available from the Making Caring Common Project at the Harvard Graduate School of Education (see Resource #11).

SOCIAL–EMOTIONAL LEARNING

Disruptions in relationships with others, emotional reactivity, and physiological arousal are common concerns for students exposed to trauma or chronic stress. Explicit teaching, combined with opportunities to apply and practice social–emotional learning (SEL) skills related to self-awareness, emotion regulation, formation and maintenance of healthy relationships, and decision-making skills, is especially critical for those students. As discussed in Chapter 3, these are also the same skills that have been shown to promote academic achievement, emotional adjustment, school engagement, and positive school behavior for all students when implemented through universal SEL programs (Durlak, Weissberg, Dymnicki, Taylor, & Schellinger, 2011). A useful guide that provides information about various SEL programs available for elementary, middle, and high school students, including target ages and grades, implementation methodology, key components, and research evidence, is available (see Resource #7). Once a school has invested in the implementation of a universal SEL program, school mental health providers can help "push-in" to classrooms with high numbers of students exposed to trauma or with high levels of behavioral problems or social conflicts to co-teach SEL lessons with educators who may need more assistance or to coach the use of SEL skills that have already been taught.

CRISIS PROTOCOLS AND PROCEDURES

When a crisis occurs in a school, the response can serve to strengthen and enhance relationships and bring the community closer together, or it can exacerbate feelings of uncertainty, fear, and disconnection. Sadly, all schools in our nation must be prepared for crisis situations ranging from deaths of students or staff (be they natural, accidental, or due to suicide or violence) to natural disasters to mass shootings. When school crises occur, any member of the school community may experience emotional or behavioral symptoms related to trauma; however, students with pre-existing trauma symptoms are particularly vulnerable to experiencing negative effects. Many resources exist to help guide schools in their creation of crisis plans and protocols, including a downloadable guide issued by the U.S. Department of Education, Office of Safe and Drug-Free Schools (2007; see Resource #5).

School mental health providers not only play an important role in designing school crisis plans in advance of a crisis, but also serve as part of the crisis team that is activated when a crisis occurs. In the wake of a crisis, a key role for school mental health providers is to assess the emotional needs of students, educators, and staff to determine what level of intervention may be required to assist with recovery. Risk factors to assess include exposure to the crisis, such as physical proximity (witness, threatened, or actual injury) and emotional proximity (relationship with the victim). In addition, previous trauma history, preexisting mental health symptoms, and lack of family or social support may also predict those who may require more support. Whereas emotional, cognitive, and physical symptoms are common in the immediate aftermath of a significant or traumatic event and typically remit with support, additional intervention may be required if they continue for more than 1 month and impair functioning. Individuals determined to be at low levels of risk for psychological symptoms related to trauma as a result of the crisis may benefit from reestablishing social support; psychoeducation about common reactions to stress, trauma, or grief; and supportive practices such as providing space for emotional reactions and expressive activities such as journaling or drawing. Those at moderate or high risk may additionally require group or individual crisis support or therapy, which are discussed in more detail in Chapters 6 and 7.

As part of their preparedness for supporting the school community in managing crisis situations, school mental health providers may find it helpful to educate themselves about Psychological First Aid for Schools (Brymer et al., 2012), a short-term, evidence-informed intervention model that can be implemented in the immediate aftermath of a schoolwide crisis to reduce immediate distress and to foster adaptive functioning and coping. Psychological First Aid for Schools includes roles for educators, families, and students as well as school mental health providers (see Exhibit 4.2).

Exhibit 4.2

Suggested Roles for School Mental Health Providers in Crisis Situations

In advance of a crisis

- Collaborate with other school personnel to prepare or revise the school crisis plan.
- Consult the *Psychological First Aid for Schools* manual (see Resource #9).

After a crisis has occurred

- Assess emotional needs and risk factors of educators, staff, and students.
- Reestablish social support networks.
- Provide psychoeducation about common reactions to stress, trauma, and loss.
- Provide space for emotional reactions and expressive activities such as journaling or art.
- Link to supportive services, including therapy, if necessary.

This approach emphasizes engaging with students, educators, and families affected by the crisis; providing immediate safety and comfort; gathering information about current needs; providing information and practical assistance; promoting social supports within the school, family, and community; providing information on coping; and linking to supportive services, including therapy, when necessary.

STUDENT SUPPORT TEAMS

Many school mental health providers are likely familiar with what has sometimes been called the "drive-by" model of school mental health consultation, in which the school mental health provider is stopped in the hallway by a principal, staff member, or teacher frustrated by a student's behavior and asked for help in "fixing" the immediate problem.

In an attempt to move to a less reactive method for supporting students and educators, schools are increasingly implementing teaming structures that can help support the MTSS model of behavioral health supports. These teams have been known by many names, including MTSS teams, student support teams, problem-solving teams, and behavioral health teams. In brief, these school-based teams are tasked with planning, implementing, and evaluating interventions at all three MTSS tiers, using data to identify students in need of support, and monitoring progress (Stephan, Sugai, Lever, & Connors, 2015). The make-up of the team varies by school but often includes an administrator, teacher, counselor, social worker, psychologist, attendance monitor, parent, and community mental health representative. A set of recommendations for establishing such teams is provided in the *School Discipline Consensus Report* (Morgan et al., 2014). The following principles guide the work of these teams:

- building on capacity and addressing needs of the individual school;
- using school data and referral and screening protocols to match students to appropriate intervention(s);
- providing evidence-based interventions that address students' social, emotional, and behavioral needs;
- collaborating with school personnel and community-based organizations to provide and/or coordinate services and form a web of support; and
- collecting, interpreting, and reporting on data to improve quality of services.

As part of a universal approach to supporting students exposed to trauma, a mechanism must exist for identifying students exposed to trauma who require more intensive levels of service. Therefore, it is recommended that schools regularly monitor student-level data, often referred to as "BAG" data (behavior, attendance, and grades) or early warning data systems (EWSs), to identify students who are demonstrating off-track indicators. In addition, teachers are on the front lines and are therefore often in the best position to identify problems early and refer students for additional support. Integrated processes for referral of students with behavioral or emotional needs, coupled with teacher training on types of student behaviors that might be indicative that more assessment or the addition of more intensive services is needed, can aid in early identification and effective use of limited resources. Within a trauma-informed framework, it is recommended that students who are identified through school-based data or teacher or staff referral as potentially requiring additional emotional or behavioral support be screened for trauma exposure and trauma symptoms as well as other mental health symptoms to ensure that traumatic exposure is considered as a potential contributor to the difficulties they are experiencing in the school setting, even in the absence of disclosure or staff knowledge about specific traumatic experiences. More information about screening and referral processes is provided in Chapter 5. When mental health needs are clearly identified, students can be matched to appropriate evidence-based interventions (such as those discussed in Chapters 6 and 7), and their progress can be monitored.

COLLABORATION WITH FAMILIES AND COMMUNITIES

Trauma occurs in a social context, and families and community members are often impacted by the very same traumas as those affecting their youth, creating both challenges and opportunities for engaging families and communities in the creation of a healing school community. Engaging families can help identify common concerns shared by school mental health providers, educators, students, families, and community members; improve the perceived relevance of school programming; and improve sensitivity to cultural factors that exist in the family and community. Providing voice and choice to those impacted by trauma, including family members, is a critical component of the trauma-informed approach articulated by SAMHSA. Recommendations include considering the role families play in the school, identifying how to share information with families, and how to build on existing family engagement efforts while ensuring that they are trauma-informed. More information on special considerations for working with families to support interventions for trauma is available in Chapter 8.

School climate, student engagement, and social connectedness can all be enhanced by building mutually beneficial partnerships with community organizations, including faith-based groups. Community organizations or individual community members can link with schools to provide mentoring, opportunities for service learning, tutoring, after-school recreational programming, and other social services for students and families that help position the school as a hub for the community that surrounds it (Weiss, Lopez, & Rosenberg, 2010). School mental health providers can help to cultivate, nurture, and support these partnerships and work to help all youth-serving adults understand the impact of trauma on youth and learn strategies for engaging and supporting these students. Another important role for school mental health providers is to actively endeavor to connect students impacted by trauma to these enrichment resources, as all too often those students who stand to benefit the most may be the least likely to seek out these resources due to factors related to their trauma histories.

CONCLUSION

Creating a trauma-informed school with all the elements described in this chapter is an enormous undertaking, one that requires coordinated efforts and dedicated leadership. Nevertheless, school mental health providers have unique expertise and knowledge that can advance progress in each of the key areas highlighted. Schools move further along the path toward becoming healing school communities with every effort made by staff to provide education about the impact of trauma on students and the importance of creating supportive relationships, build students' social emotional learning skills, provide support and guidance in the aftermath of a school crisis, and create collaborative relationships with families and community partners. The Resources section at the end of the book has a number of useful links and guides to support your efforts.

5

Preintervention Strategies for School Mental Health Providers

In Chapters 6 and 7, you will read about Tier 2 and Tier 3 evidence-based treatments available for schools that can provide needed support to trauma-exposed students. Although it may be tempting to begin implementing an intervention to get students support as quickly as possible, several preintervention strategies can set you up for success over the course of implementing school-based interventions for trauma. This chapter focuses on concrete strategies that are necessary prior to implementing universal or targeted trauma intervention in schools. We discuss administrator support, partnership with teachers, outreach to families, screening tools and strategies, and logistical considerations.

http://dx.doi.org/10.1037/0000072-006
Creating Healing School Communities: School-Based Interventions for Students Exposed to Trauma,
by C. D. Santiago, T. Raviv, and L. H. Jaycox
Copyright © 2018 by the American Psychological Association. All rights reserved.

ADMINISTRATOR SUPPORT

Ensuring support from principals and other administrators is critical to the success and sustainability of trauma-informed support for students. In fact, lack of buy-in and support from administrators has been identified as a key barrier to implementing a school-based intervention for trauma (Langley, Nadeem, Kataoka, Stein, & Jaycox, 2010). On the other hand, school mental health providers who were able to implement the program noted that their principals were supportive and open to the program (Langley et al., 2010). School-based providers will find it critical to partner with administrators before and during the implementation of a school-based intervention.

Whereas some principals may understand the effect of trauma on students and encourage training in and implementation of interventions for traumas, some school mental health providers may need to educate others on the effects of trauma. The National Child Traumatic Stress Network (NCTSN; 2008) *Trauma Toolkit for Educators* provides a good starting point for beginning a conversation about the impact of trauma on students. School mental health providers can share the toolkit's fact sheets with principals and other administrators as a way to begin a conversation about the need for school-based interventions for trauma. Providing an in-service training for teachers and administrators may be another way to share key information. These efforts can be part of a universal intervention approach or build on such efforts. For example, providing "Trauma 101" as discussed in Chapter 4 can improve school climate and sensitivity to trauma as well as increase support for Tier 2 interventions. Another resource that can aid school mental health providers in increasing awareness of trauma is the "Students and Trauma" DVD that includes perspectives of students, teachers, and administrators (see Resource #12 in the Resources section at the end of this book).

In addition to increasing awareness of trauma and the need for school-based interventions to address trauma, it may also be important to consider how the intervention might fit into existing structures and school contexts. As discussed in Chapter 3, several efforts within schools align well with implementing interventions for trauma within schools. First, the emphasis on social–emotional learning within schools is growing. Second, the Multi-Tiered System of Supports (MTSS) model provides a framework for delivering interventions within schools. In partnering with school administrators, school mental health providers may find it helpful to discuss how an intervention fits within the MTSS framework and could support students' social and emotional development to increase buy-in and support for the program. Finally, it is particularly important to highlight for administrators the documented link between improvements in students' social emotional functioning and the academic outcomes on which school (and administrator) performance are judged.

PARTNERING WITH TEACHERS

Teachers are on the front lines of work with students. To accurately identify students who may have been exposed to trauma or whose behaviors in the classroom raise concerns, teachers must be educated both on signs and symptoms that might signal underlying trauma as well as on how and when to seek additional support from school mental health providers. In one study assessing teachers' experiences with a school-based intervention for trauma, teachers consistently reported wanting more trauma education and tools to identify students affected by trauma (Baweja et al., 2016). In addition to the NCTSN (2008) *Trauma Toolkit for Educators*, another helpful resource is *Listen, Protect, Connect—Model & Teach: Psychological First Aid (PFA) for Students and Teachers* (Schreiber, Gurwitch, & Wong, 2006) published by the U.S. Department of Homeland Security (see Resource #13). This resource provides information on traumatic stress and clear and simple strategies for supporting students following a traumatic event. These types of resources as well as presentations and in-services can increase awareness of trauma among teachers and ultimately improve referrals for school-based interventions.

In addition to sharing information with teachers before implementing a school-based intervention, it is important to work collaboratively as you plan the logistics of the intervention. Overall, teachers tend to be supportive of mental health programs for trauma (e.g., Baweja et al., 2016), but they also note concerns about balancing academic needs and instruction time. Including teachers in problem-solving scheduling concerns can increase teacher buy-in and program sustainability (Langley, Santiago,

Rodríguez, & Zelaya, 2013). Offering intervention sessions during non-academic periods or during lunch, or rotating which academic period is missed each week, are often good compromises for balancing academic and mental health needs for students.

OUTREACH TO FAMILIES

Prior to implementing a school-based intervention, increasing parent or caregiver awareness of available services can pave the way for successful partnership during an intervention. As noted in Chapter 3 of this volume, stigma can be a major barrier to seeking services (McKay & Bannon, 2004). Providing services in schools is more acceptable to families, and school-based providers can take additional steps to reduce stigma and increase awareness about programs.

Many schools hold "Back to School" events or other open house or informational sessions for caregivers. These types of events provide an opportunity to familiarize caregivers with available school-based programs for trauma. Having a table at these events can provide an informal way for students and caregivers to learn about existing programs in a destigmatizing and familiar atmosphere. Including information about interventions in school newsletters and publications can also increase familiarity with available interventions. Finally, caregivers themselves represent a key resource for other caregivers. Many caregivers who have students in the school-based trauma interventions report high levels of satisfaction (Santiago et al., 2013). Often caregivers report wishing they had known about the program sooner and stating that they would recommend the program to other caregivers (Santiago, Fuller, Lennon, & Kataoka, 2016). It may be helpful to partner with caregivers who are interested in recommending the program to other families at school events so they can share a caregiver perspective. Some schools also have parent leaders and advocates who may also be willing to help raise awareness for existing programs. These types of strategies may increase caregiver referrals for services but also provide a foundation for partnering with caregivers during an intervention. Caregivers who are already familiar with a program may be more open to providing consent and being involved in the treatment. We discuss caregiver consent and additional engagement strategies for involving caregivers during treatment in Chapter 8.

SCREENING AND IDENTIFYING STUDENTS

Whereas universal interventions are delivered schoolwide or to whole classrooms, Tier 2 interventions are used with students who have been identified as needing more targeted services. Prior to beginning a Tier 2 intervention, school mental health providers need a process for obtaining referrals and screening students for eligibility. Parent nomination, teacher referral, and broader screening are all approaches that can be considered for identifying students in need of services. These approaches differ greatly in their feasibility, level of effort, and validity, however, and thus the method of identification should be considered carefully. Whereas the universal screening approach is likely to identify many more underserved and needy students, the process is time-consuming and requires substantial effort. In this section, we describe each method.

Screening and Referral Process

There are numerous ways to identify students who may be eligible for a Tier 2 trauma-focused intervention. Considering existing school resources and protocols is helpful in determining which strategies best fit your school. Many school-based providers rely on teachers and other staff (e.g., nurses) for referrals, while parent or caregiver nomination is another important referral source. As mentioned in the preceding section, increasing teacher awareness of trauma can increase referrals. Other times, school mental health providers receive referrals for concerns other than trauma (e.g., behavioral problems, withdrawal). These types of problems sometimes surface after students have been exposed to traumatic events. For this reason, many school mental health providers review their existing caseloads to identify students who have trauma exposure and qualify for a Tier 2 intervention. Other school districts may have behavioral health teams or similar units (as discussed in Chapter 4) where teachers and mental health providers work together to identify student social–emotional needs and intervention approaches. These types of teams can naturally support referrals and screening for Tier 2 interventions.

A drawback to these methods, however, is that they might miss students who are struggling with trauma-related problems who are "flying under the radar" and are not being seen by mental health providers; students whose depression and anxiety are related to trauma might also be overlooked by teachers and parents, who are much more likely to notice students with acting out and disruptive behaviors. Therefore, broader screening is required to identify students who may benefit from Tier 2. For example, some schools conduct more universal screening of entire classrooms or grade levels. In a recent study that conducted universal screenings of elementary students, 34% of students screened had been exposed to a traumatic event and 26% reported posttraumatic stress disorder (PTSD) symptoms in the moderate range or higher (Gonzalez, Monzon, Solis, Jaycox, & Langley, 2016). These findings suggest that many more students in need of treatment may be identified through a broader screening approach compared with relying on teacher observations and referrals alone. Many students may meet eligibility criteria for a Tier 2 intervention before exhibiting clear academic or behavioral difficulties. Intervening before these difficulties develop may prevent a more serious decline in functioning. However, before embarking on a universal screening approach, schools must also consider the capacity to meet the needs of identified students. For example, if a school mental health provider will be responsible for conducting a Tier 2 intervention and has the time to implement one group intervention with six students during the year, then screening an entire grade level would likely be inappropriate.

When an appropriate screening and referral approach is identified, school policies related to consent for screening must be considered. Some schools require caregiver consent prior to conducting any mental health screening, while other schools do not require a special consent for screening. When parental consent is needed, mailing consent forms for screening with general school enrollment paperwork has proven to be an effective means for getting parental authorization. Other strategies include sending consent forms in student backpacks, with school newsletters, or with other school communication. See Chapter 8 for additional caregiver consent considerations.

Screening Measures

Screening students using standardized measures is critical: It ensures that students are matched to the appropriate types of services, and it provides a data point that can help monitor progress of students over the course of the intervention. No single standard, widely used universal screener is recommended, but several options are available (see Exhibit 5.1). For

---

Exhibit 5.1

Examples of Screening Instruments

Trauma Exposure
- Life Events Checklist (B. Singer, Ryff, Carr, & Magee, 1998; M. I. Singer, Anglin, Song, & Lunghofer, 1995)
  - Used with school-age children and adolescents exposed to community violence
- UCLA PTSD Reaction Index (Pynoos et al., 1998)
  - Contains 12 items that assess exposure to natural disaster, accident, violence, and medical trauma
- Traumatic Events Screening Inventory for Children (Ford et al., 2000)
  - Used with children ages 6–17 years

PTSD Symptoms
- Child PTSD Symptom Scale (Foa et al., 2001; Gillihan et al., 2013)
  - Score of 14 or more is typically used as a cut-off point for inclusion in a Tier 2
- UCLA PTSD Reaction Index (Pynoos et al., 1998)
  - Score of 20 or above is typically used for inclusion in a Tier 2 intervention

Other Domains of Functioning
- Child Depression Inventory (Kovacs, 1985)
- Strengths and Difficulties Questionnaire (Goodman, 1997)

Note. UCLA = University of California, Los Angeles; PTSD = posttraumatic stress disorder.

---

trauma-focused interventions, screening is typically a two-step process: students are first screened for exposure to traumatic events, and then they are screened for elevated PTSD symptoms. Appropriate screening depends a good deal on the age of the child—children ages 8 years and older can often be screened independently, whereas screening younger children will usually include parent input.

Numerous instruments can be used for screening for exposure to traumatic events. An extensive database of information about screening instruments, including cost, instructions on how to access, and languages available, is maintained by the National Child Traumatic Stress Network (Resource #32). Here, we highlight several options that demonstrate good reliability and validity for use with school-age children or adolescents. A modified version of the Life Events Checklist (B. Singer, Ryff, Carr, & Magee, 1998; M. I. Singer, Anglin, Song, & Lunghofer, 1995) has been used extensively to screen for trauma exposure, including community violence, especially in the context of implementing the Cognitive Behavioral Intervention for Trauma in Schools (Jaycox, 2003). Another option is to use the University of California, Los Angeles (UCLA) PTSD Reaction Index (Pynoos, Rodriguez, Steinberg, Stuber, & Frederick, 1998), which contains 12 items that assess lifetime trauma exposures, including natural disaster, accident, violence, and medical trauma. In addition, the Traumatic Events Screening Inventory for Children—Brief Form (Ford et al., 2000) has been used with youth ages 6 to 17 representing a good range for school-based screening across elementary, middle, and high schools.

It is important to consider whether to screen for sexual abuse. Because many Tier 2 interventions are delivered in a group format, some school mental health providers remove sexual abuse from screening instruments, as it is typically not appropriate to treat trauma from sexual abuse in a group setting with a range of types of trauma exposure. Other school-based providers include sexual abuse on screeners and refer for Tier 3 interventions (e.g., individual trauma-focused therapy) if endorsed. Finally, it is also important to consider the context and type of intervention that is planned. For example, a more specific measure such as the Disaster Experiences Questionnaire (Scheeringa, 2005) may be appropriate if you are forming a group in response to a recent hurricane or other natural disaster that has affected an entire school community.

Several screening measures are available to screen for elevated PTSD symptoms among school-age children and adolescents. The Child PTSD Symptom Scale (Foa, Johnson, Feeny, & Treadwell, 2001; Gillihan, Aderka, Conklin, Capaldi, & Foa, 2013) has been widely used with youth in school settings (e.g., Kataoka et al., 2003; Stein et al., 2003). For this measure, a sum score of 14 or more, indicative of moderate levels of symptoms, is typically used as a cutoff point for inclusion in a Tier 2 intervention such as Cognitive Behavioral Intervention for Trauma in Schools. The UCLA PTSD Reaction Index (Pynoos et al., 1998) is another well-validated measure that has been used with children as young as age 7. Scores in the 20-to-25 range are considered indicative of moderate PTSD symptoms (and inclusion in a Tier 2 intervention; Langley et al., 2015).

In addition to screening for trauma exposure and PTSD symptoms, it may be helpful to include supplemental measures of depression and more general emotional and behavioral functioning. Though these may not be necessary for screening for inclusion in a Tier 2 intervention, they can provide additional clinical information and another opportunity to compare pre- and postintervention scores; some evidence suggests that many trauma interventions also improve symptoms of anxiety and depression. The Child Depression Inventory has strong psychometric properties and has been widely used with children ages 7 through 17 (Kovacs, 1985). The Strengths and Difficulties Questionnaire (Goodman, 1997; Goodman, Meltzer, & Bailey, 1998) is a good option when attempting to assess a broader range of functioning and to obtain teacher or parent perspectives. The questionnaire has a teacher and parent version and has been translated into a number of languages, including Spanish (see http://www.sdqinfo.com).

Administration Recommendations

Careful administration of these screening measures will help to ensure student comprehension and accurate measurement of symptoms. Older students may benefit from having a measure read aloud, while marking responses on their own copy of the measure. For elementary students, administering questionnaires verbally is extremely important. Younger children may have difficulty reading the questionnaires themselves and comprehending the language of the questionnaires. By administering the measures verbally, reading difficulty is no longer a barrier. As recommended by Gonzalez and colleagues (2016), school mental health providers can gauge comprehension by asking for definitions of key terms (e.g., violence, threatened) and define terms that children do not understand. Furthermore, school mental health providers should provide concrete examples of items; children may say no to broad prompts but be able to understand and report trauma exposure to more specific examples. Finally, school mental health providers may need to ask follow-up questions to determine if an event happened in "real life" to the child (as opposed to being seen on TV or reporting an event that happened to someone the child knows; Gonzalez et al., 2016). Using visual aids for responses can also increase valid reporting. For example, school mental health providers can use pictures of feelings thermometers or simple cylinders that range from empty (e.g., not at all) to full (e.g., a lot). Parent or caregiver report of child trauma exposure and child functioning can also supplement child self-report. For younger children, a caregiver's report may help to confirm child report when the screening was difficult for the child to understand. However, in some cases, caregivers may underestimate child exposure to trauma and distress; caregivers typically have a harder time reporting on their child's internalizing symptoms as compared with externalizing or behavioral problems (De Los Reyes & Kazdin, 2005). A relaxation exercise or brief check-in after completing screening can help transition students back into their school day after completing a screening measure.

FUNDING

Those working in schools are aware that funding for school mental health is inadequate to meet the needs in many communities. Therefore, schools and community mental health agencies must work collaboratively to leverage existing funding and seek new funding opportunities. Often referred to as "braided funding," most solutions to funding challenges involve using several sources of funding. The most common sources of funding for school-based services include federal grants, state funding, fee-for-service reimbursements through private or public insurance, and solicited funds from private donors or foundations (S. W. Evans et al., 2003). Using a combination of funding sources can ensure that funding is secured for activities beyond "face to face" time spent with a mental health professional, such as consultation with teachers, screening, case management, documentation, planning, and training in specific interventions. The Technical Assistance Partnership for Child and Family Mental Health issued a helpful guide, which includes successful strategies, examples of school mental health funding formulas, Medicaid resources, and sample contracts (Resource #31).

ADDITIONAL PLANNING CONSIDERATIONS

In addition to forming partnerships and identifying students for a Tier 2 intervention, school mental health providers also need to plan for timing of groups and space for groups. Partnering with teachers is important as school mental health providers plan for timing of groups. Offering intervention sessions during nonacademic periods, during lunch, and rotating which academic period is missed each week are often good strategies for scheduling groups. If the group will not occur on a consistent day and time, it is important to provide participants with a schedule and to implement a system for reminding students about the group to provide predictability and minimize missed groups caused by scheduling confusion. Finding appropriate space for group can also be a challenge, especially in schools with limited resources. A space that provides privacy and confidentiality as well as room to accommodate group members is needed. For younger students, a room with space to sit in a circle on the floor may be best, whereas arranging chairs in a circle or sitting around a table may work well for older students. Offices, empty classrooms, or meeting rooms typically work well. In our experience, having a predictable and consistent space for group is important for promoting students' feelings of safety. Problem solving with an administrator may be necessary in schools with limited spaces. Finally, as school mental health providers receive referrals and screen to form groups, they should consider factors such as age, gender, cognitive ability, and social functioning in group composition. Typically, groups comprising students in the same grade or within one grade level (e.g., sixth and seventh graders) are suitable. Mixed gender groups often work well as long as there is a balance of both genders. Finally, clinical judgment is necessary to determine whether a student has the cognitive and social ability to participate in a group format intervention.

CONCLUSION

Prior to implementing a school-based intervention for trauma, school mental health providers should consider several important issues. Building key partnerships with administrators, teachers, and caregivers provides a solid foundation for getting support throughout the intervention and increasing referrals and collaboration. Selecting an appropriate screening strategy that fits within the school context is also a key first step. Careful selection and administration of screening measures support group formation and enable tracking student outcomes (e.g., pre- to postintervention comparison). With some thoughtful planning, school mental health providers can ensure their implementation of a trauma-focused intervention is set up for success.

6

Common Evidence-Based Treatment Components

In line with evidence-based treatments for individuals affected by trauma (Foa et al., 2008), most school-based interventions use a set of core cognitive behavioral components to reduce symptoms of posttraumatic stress disorder and depression and to improve long-term coping with stress and trauma. Although many people are resilient and can recover from a traumatic experience over time, a substantial minority do not recover and feel some lasting effects of the event, warranting intervention. The concepts of what gets in the way of recovery are spelled out most fully for adults (Rauch & Foa, 2006) but apply very well to children. These underlying impediments to recovery drive the intervention techniques that are included in most school-based interventions. Table 6.1 lists some of the common techniques used to address each of these impediments (Cohen, Mannarino, & Deblinger; 2006; Jaycox, Kataoka, Stein, Langley, & Wong,

http://dx.doi.org/10.1037/0000072-007
Creating Healing School Communities: School-Based Interventions for Students Exposed to Trauma,
by C. D. Santiago, T. Raviv, and L. H. Jaycox
Copyright © 2018 by the American Psychological Association. All rights reserved.

Table 6.1

Evidence-Based Intervention Techniques and Their Contributions to Recovery

Intervention technique	Contribution to recovery from trauma
Psychoeducation	Trauma reactions can be poorly understood by trauma survivors and the people in their support system. Psychoeducation can help people understand trauma reactions, instill hope for recovery, and restore a sense of control following trauma.
Recognition of maladaptive thinking Challenging maladaptive thoughts and beliefs	Perceptions and cognitions can change following trauma, particularly ideas about yourself ("I am weak" or "I am alone") and about the world ("People can't be trusted" or "The world is dangerous"). Cognitive restructuring helps to develop more adaptive ways of thinking ("I can be strong, I can be safe").
Relaxation training Emotion regulation Mindfulness	During a traumatic event, an individual learns that the event and associated characteristics (e.g., location, type of person, time of day) are dangerous. Trauma reminders can therefore result in a great deal of anxiety. These techniques train people to reduce anxiety when it occurs.
Safety planning Challenging unrealistic thoughts and beliefs	Risk for additional trauma exposure is high for some people. These techniques help people make accurate judgments about their safety in different situations.
In vivo exposure to trauma reminders (intentional approach rather than avoidance of reminders)	The natural reaction to anxiety is to try to diminish it, but avoiding trauma reminders serves to increase and maintain the anxiety over time. In vivo exposure helps people do the things they need and want to do and to feel more effective and confident while doing so.
Development of a trauma narrative Imaginal exposure to the trauma memory	Memories of traumatic events and traumatic loss can be fragmented and can include a lot of negative emotions. Focusing and processing the trauma makes them more like the other kinds of memories we have.
Developing peer and parent support Social problem solving	The recovery process can put a strain on personal relationships and the ability to handle everyday stress. These techniques help with daily problems and build hope for the future.
Development of a trauma narrative Imaginal exposure to the trauma memory Enhancement of positive memories of those lost Grief work	When a loved one is lost in a traumatic manner, it can be difficult to remember the person without triggering frightening memories of and reactions to the traumatic death. These techniques help foster the bereavement processes such as coping with grief, remembering and memorializing the deceased, and forming new relationships.

2012; Jaycox, Langley, Stein, Kataoka, & Wong, 2014), and these techniques are described in more detail in the following sections.

PSYCHOEDUCATION

Interventions often begin with some education about common reactions to traumatic events. Despite growing recognition of trauma and its impact, the general public is still poorly informed about the exact symptoms and may not realize that a symptom is connected to trauma. For instance, child sleep problems may be seen by parents as a difficult and annoying problem, but they may not realize that it is directly connected to the trauma experience. In fact, the screening and consent/assent processes begin by informing students and caregivers that people who experience trauma or traumatic loss generally also experience a specific set of problems related to that trauma and that interventions are available to support recovery. Psychoeducation explains common reactions to trauma, provides an explanation of how the recovery process works, and offers hope for the future. Common reactions discussed include cognitions (e.g., the world is dangerous), physical reactions (e.g., stomachaches, headaches), behaviors (e.g., avoidance of traumatic reminders), and strong feelings (e.g., anger, exaggerated startle). Some interventions, such as Structured Psychotherapy for Adolescents Responding to Chronic Stress (DeRosa & Pelcovitz, 2009), also emphasize reactions that are common to chronic stress or interpersonal trauma, such as risk behaviors, self-harm, and problems in relationships. In most of the trauma-focused interventions the focus is on symptoms of posttraumatic stress disorder, and therefore the entire range of those symptoms are also included.

An advantage of intervention groups in schools is that the discussion of these common problems brings students together and makes them feel less isolated and alone. Similarly, including caregivers or other family members in treatment helps to connect the dots and make these family supports more in tune with the traumatized child and thus able to be more supportive. Similarly, a teacher who understands the classroom manifestations of trauma is likely to be more empathic when a child has trouble concentrating, startles at a loud noise, or acts up in class. Psychoeducation may take the form of discussion, handouts, and video and slide presentations. In the Cognitive Behavioral Intervention for Trauma in Schools (CBITS; Jaycox, 2003) program, for example, a discussion is conducted in the student group meetings with three goals: (a) to normalize the common symptoms that students are experiencing, (b) to explain how the CBITS course can help with each of them, and (c) to provide hope that these problems will lessen over time. The students bring a handout home to caregivers and are assigned the task of showing the caregiver which ones apply to them. This information is also included in the CBITS parent information session. CBITS provides a training session to teachers that explains the common reactions and also suggests tips for working with traumatized students in the classroom.

RELAXATION AND EMOTION REGULATION SKILLS

Another common element to school interventions related to trauma are to teach relaxation to directly combat the posttrauma anxiety that most children experience. Slow, even breathing (also known as diaphragmatic breathing), progressive muscle relaxation, and positive imagery are all potential techniques, and training on more than one can be helpful so that students can find a relaxation method that works best for them. Use of more physically engaged relaxation techniques, such as yoga or stretching, can also work well for some youth. A key element is to encourage practice—either by doing some relaxation in each meeting or by encouraging outside practice and checking on how it is working. Many teens and tweens also report success with applications they can download onto their phones or tablets, such as Breathe2Relax (National Center for Telehealth and Technology, 2017), that can help coach them through a relaxation strategy, track stress levels before and after, provide reminders to practice, and be accompanied by soothing music or images.

Other techniques at self-regulation include thought stopping (saying "stop" or snapping a rubber band when noticing a particular repetitive maladaptive thought), increasing positive activities to increase positive affect, and using distraction. Finally, distress tolerance techniques, originating out of dialectical behavior therapy (e.g., Linehan, 1993), can help youth cope in more adaptive ways with intense emotions. Self-care and self-soothing techniques include encouraging youth to perform small acts of kindness for themselves, with an emphasis on relaxing sensory experiences such as taking a bubble bath, putting on lotion, or drinking a cup of tea or hot chocolate. Other examples of distress tolerance techniques include seeking out experiences that provoke opposing emotions (e.g., watching a comedy, listening to upbeat music), helping someone else, focusing on other tasks or thoughts, or creating a sadness or worry "box" where you write down distressing thoughts or feelings and symbolically "put them in the box" to mentally set them aside.

MINDFULNESS

Mindfulness practices strive to increase awareness and the ability to attend to experiences occurring in the present moment in a sustained and receptive fashion, without judgment. The practice is rooted in Eastern contemplative traditions, such as yoga and meditation, which have been shown to have both physical and mental health benefits when practiced regularly. Although related to relaxation and stress management techniques commonly included in cognitive behavior therapy (CBT) interventions, mindfulness practices are distinct, and more commonly found in dialectical behavior therapy interventions. Research with adult trauma survivors has led to increased use of mindfulness techniques with traumatized adolescents, and mindfulness training is included in some trauma interventions for adolescents that have been used in schools, such as Structured Psychotherapy for Adolescents Responding to Chronic Stress (DeRosa & Pelcovitz, 2009) and Trauma Adaptive Recovery Group Education and Therapy for Adolescents (Ford, Mahoney, & Russo, 2001).

For traumatized youth, mindfulness techniques have three goals: to improve affect regulation/reduce reactivity, to reduce somatic symptoms by regulating stress response systems, and to improve self-acceptance. Techniques taught to youth focus on being fully aware in the moment, such as by paying attention to sensory experiences and describing these experiences in detail. Distractions occur naturally and can be external (noises, other people) or internal (thoughts). While engaging in mindfulness activities, youth are taught to notice these distractions and bring attention and awareness back to the mindfulness practice. An important component of mindfulness is being nonjudgmental of the thoughts, feelings, and behaviors that occur during mindfulness practice, as well as those that have occurred at other times.

Like relaxation, cultivating mindfulness requires practice. Also, different techniques are effective for different youth, so introducing them to different techniques to try is encouraged. Many resources for mindfulness activities for individuals or groups of youth can be found online. Jon Kabat-Zinn, a renowned researcher and developer of the Mindfulness-Based Stress Reduction program, even has recordings of guided meditation available on youtube.com. The Committee for Children (2016) recently released Mind Yeti, a free application designed to teach mindfulness to elementary school children as a complement to the Second Step social–emotional learning curriculum (see Resource #16 in the Resources section at the end of this book).

COGNITIVE SKILL BUILDING

The cognitive component of trauma-focused CBT includes identifying irrational, unrealistic, or maladaptive thinking and then challenging that thinking, with the goal of reaching a more adaptive or helpful perspective on the problem. This is a general set of skills that are proven to be helpful for a variety of depressive and anxiety disorders, and thus can be useful for many children following a traumatic event. Some common examples of dysfunctional thinking following a traumatic event include self-blame (or an inflated sense of responsibility for the event or something that happened during it), a sense of being unable to cope or handle things (often caused by the posttrauma symptoms being experienced), and an exaggerated sense of dangerousness or inability to trust other people.

Children are taught to see a link between thoughts and feelings such that the feelings usually match the underlying thoughts and beliefs. Identification of such maladaptive thoughts and beliefs can be taught to students in a variety of ways, including individual work to review recent situations that provoked strong emotional reactions, use of short surveys that assess frequency or trauma-related maladaptive thoughts, and group exercises that elicit different possible thoughts in a scenario and then matching emotional reactions to each.

Next, students are taught to challenge the problematic thinking by evaluating alternatives and evidence for the thoughts, and considering consequences (both positive and negative) or plan of action if the thought is accurate (see Table 6.2). The following questions can be used to challenge maladaptive thinking: "What evidence do I have that this is true?" "Are there other ways to think about this?" "What is the worst/best/ most likely outcome?" "If this is true, what can I do about it?" Challenging maladaptive thoughts can be done using worksheets or interactive games. For example, the developers of trauma-focused CBT created a free application called Triangle of Life (Allegheny Health Network, 2015), a game that allows the player to practice identifying and challenging negative thoughts. A goal with this cognitive component is to train this skill such that youth more readily recognize the maladaptive thoughts they are having and learn to challenge maladaptive thinking more automatically. This skill is usually taught early in therapy and practiced throughout the course of the therapy.

Table 6.2
Examples of Maladaptive and Helpful Thinking

Maladaptive, unrealistic thought	Possible helpful thoughts
"I'll never feel better."	"I'm working on feeling better."
	"Some days are better than others."
	"I can talk to my mom about it—that usually helps."
"I can't trust anyone."	"I can trust a few people and will try to spend more time with them."
	"I believe this because of what happened and can try to build trusting relationships now."
"It is unsafe everywhere."	"I am safe at home."
	"It feels unsafe, but I see other people like me around and they seem to be safe."
	"I feel unsafe because I'm anxious, and can check with someone to see if it is really unsafe."

CREATION OF A TRAUMA NARRATIVE
AND IMAGINAL EXPOSURE

Directly working on the traumatic memory itself is also an important component of most of the trauma-focused therapies. Although the methods vary (e.g., drawing, writing, sharing verbally), the purpose is similar: to have the child deliberately expose himself or herself to the trauma memory so as to process it, form a more coherent, less fragmented memory of it, identify problematic interpretations about it, and develop additional support from parents and/or peers. For extremely anxious students, the relaxation and mindfulness techniques discussed earlier can be used to reduce anxiety during and after this type of trauma work.

Remember Sydnee from Chapter 2? This 15-year-old survived Hurricane Katrina and was having many symptoms of posttraumatic stress disorder, including nightmares, concerns about safety of family members, sleep problems, and concentration problems. Some of her symptoms, like feeling that the hurricane is happening again when there is a thunderstorm and intrusive thinking about the hurricane, indicate that she has not fully processed the trauma.

When Sydnee's teacher referred her to the school social worker, she began trauma-focused cognitive behavior therapy. This included relaxation skills and learning to recognize and challenge irrational, unrealistic thoughts. Specifically, she learned to notice when she had concerns about family members' safety and to counteract them with ideas like, "I'm worrying for no reason—they will be fine." In therapy, she focused on the hurricane trauma experience itself by talking about it with the therapist in great detail several times and writing a letter about it to share with her mother. Although she was very nervous at the beginning of talking about it and when reading the letter to her mother, she calmed down by the end of each experience and learned that she could think about it without losing control. By the end of therapy, her nightmares and intrusive thoughts about the trauma had diminished. Her teachers reported better attention in class.

This aspect of school trauma interventions is the most unfamiliar to many school mental health professionals, especially those who have no prior training in these methods. Many are trained to wait until a child is "ready" to address trauma or abuse rather than directing them to do so. But with the proper framing and explanation of why this is important to do, most if not all students are able to readily address their traumas head-on. Success in this is a boost to confidence and helps to counteract the idea that many children hold that they aren't strong enough to confront their trauma or that the trauma is too awful to share.

IN VIVO EXPOSURE

Exposure to trauma reminders commonly creates anxiety and distress, and the in vivo exposure component is intended to directly address that. By approaching, rather than avoiding, trauma reminders, and sticking with the situation long enough for habituation to occur and anxiety to be reduced, children are able to see that their anxiety will not last forever and that they can handle these reminders. The relaxation and mindfulness skills described earlier can be used to make this work easier for students. This component is most easily accomplished with a fair amount of parental buy-in and support because parents often have to help the child access the situation and must understand the rationale so that they don't inadvertently avoid the situation themselves. In particular, parents often either have shared the traumatic experience with the child and are thus avoidant themselves, or worry for their child and can be overly protective in the aftermath of a trauma. One key factor in this component is to ensure that the children are choosing situations that are traumatic reminders but that are not actually dangerous, and this assessment of safety is an important skill in itself. Sometimes children are not particularly avoidant of trauma reminders, and in these cases this component is a little bit less important. However, there is often some social anxiety and behavioral avoidance—many, if not most, students will have some things that they avoid due to anxiety—and this component can help address that.

To address avoidance, the first step is to list the reminders or activities and rate them in terms of the amount of anxiety they would create if

Table 6.3

Example of a Fear Hierarchy for a Student Who Witnesses a Drive-By Shooting on His Way to the Corner Grocery Store at Dusk

Situation or reminder	Anxiety rating
Walking to the corner grocery at dusk, alone	10
Walking to the corner grocery at dusk, with parent	8
Walking around the block at dusk, with parent	7
Walking around the block at dusk, alone	6
Walking around the block in the morning, alone	5
Walking around the block in the morning, with parent	4

Note. Anxiety rating scale: 0 = *no anxiety*; 10 = *extreme anxiety*.

encountered (typically on a 0–10 scale). Then, the student would pick an item from the list (or hierarchy) that causes a low- to mid-level amount of anxiety (like a 3 or a 4), work on it until it becomes easy to do, and then move to a more difficult item on the hierarchy. As the student works and gains confidence, the items high on the list get easier to face, so the student is never approaching something seen as extremely anxiety-provoking. An example of a typical fear hierarchy is provided in Table 6.3.

SAFETY PLANNING

Another key component in working with students exposed to trauma is safety planning. For some students, such as those exposed to violence at home or in their neighborhoods, there is an ongoing threat of additional violence, and they need help to come up with strategies to reduce their risk. For others, the risk of additional trauma is relatively low but their anxiety and cognitive distortions make it difficult for them to judge what is safe and what is dangerous. Some of these students may begin to engage in risky behaviors; others may be very avoidant and withdrawn. In either case, working with the student to determine what are relatively safe and normal activities can be helpful. Students can ask themselves the following questions: "Are other kids like me doing that/going there?" "Are there people around that I could go to if something goes wrong?" "Would my mother/father/parent be comfortable with me doing this?"

GRIEF AND LOSS

Many traumatic events also include some element of loss, and thus a student might be grieving in addition to experiencing anxiety or posttraumatic stress disorder symptoms. The trauma narrative can provide some entry into the processing of a traumatic loss, but it focuses more on the anxiety-related aspects than the loss itself. Thus, separate work on grief can sometimes be necessary.

Such techniques involve creating books or projects that include memories of the deceased, writing letters to the deceased, finding ways to remember the positives of the individual when alive rather than the memories of them very ill or dead, and finding new rituals within the family that honor and remember the one they lost.

Remember William from Chapter 2? He had witnessed a car accident and his sister's death, and he was experiencing a lot of somatic symptoms, avoidance of walking to and from school, and withdrawal from peers and activities. His parents were worried that he was becoming depressed. Working with a therapist, William first began learning ways to manage his worry and fear about walking to school, and his therapist asked him to do activities that he used to find fun even though he wasn't enjoying them at present. She suggested that he and his parents use graded in vivo exposure techniques to begin walking to school again, starting with one parent walking with him on a weekend, and gradually working up to him doing it alone on a school day. As he began to feel a bit more in control of his daily activities, he also began working directly on the trauma by talking with the therapist about witnessing the car accident and creating a picture of it in one of the therapy sessions. He created a memory book about his sister and wrote her a letter saying how much he missed her. Sharing this with his parents was the first time they had really talked about her death together, and it provided an opportunity for them to support one another. Because he was having repeated thoughts of his sister lying in the casket, the therapist also suggested that he find a picture of her alive and healthy and to keep it handy, so that he could look at that when he remembered the disturbing image.

After a few weeks of therapy, William reported feeling a little bit more confident and able to carry out normal activities, though still feeling sad much of the time as well. His somatic symptoms improved, and he got his appetite back. He asked his parents if they could visit his sister's grave, and they decided to do this as a family once a week, at least for a while. Teachers reported that William seemed more at ease and was attending class regularly again.

SOCIAL PROBLEM-SOLVING

Some of the school interventions include some problem-solving components to help address the real-life problems that many traumatized children face. Addressing the cognitions and behaviors of traumatized students will not solve the issues of ongoing community violence, familial conflict, or bullying, for example. Therefore, some basic skill building related to brainstorming solutions and assessing the pros and cons of various options can help for some of these daily problems. As an example, consider one problem faced by children exposed to community violence: It might not be safe to walk to school, yet they need to on a daily basis. In cases like this, brainstorming and weighing pros and cons might lead the students to start a walk-to-school program in their community. School-based mental health professionals can help the students come up with ideas, link them to the proper resources (including community leaders), and set them on a path toward addressing real-life problems.

Remember Kenneth from Chapter 2? He had experienced domestic violence, physical abuse, unstable housing, and community violence. His behavior had come to the attention of his mother and teachers, and he was getting in trouble at school. The school counselor was aware of his trauma history and began to work with him on emotion regulation skills. Specifically, she taught Kenneth how to notice his thoughts that were driving his anger and how to slow down the process by taking deep breaths and coming up with alternative ways of interpreting the situation. At the same time, she worked with him to identify ways to act that might be more acceptable in school, so that instead of leaving the classroom or being aggressive, he found a way to stay and talk to the teacher afterward. In discussions with Kenneth, she learned that one classroom in particular was difficult for him because a student in there would tease him about being homeless. After that problem was identified, they worked with the teacher to control that in the classroom, and the teacher gave Kenneth the option of changing seats and also asking for a bathroom pass if he needed a short break.

Over time, Kenneth's behavior improved a bit in school, and the counselor told him that interventions were available to help students work on trauma. He decided to join the next trauma group, starting in a few weeks.

CAREGIVER COMPONENTS

In school-based interventions for trauma, there are varying degrees of caregiver involvement. In Bounce Back, for early elementary students, caregivers are involved at all stages of the intervention, and in particular, at the beginning and during the development of the trauma narrative. Sometimes caregivers of older students can be difficult to reach or engage with the interventions. However, whenever possible, it is important to try to engage caregivers and work with them on some of these same components. In many cases the caregivers have been traumatized themselves, and therefore can benefit from the CBT skills directly, and in other cases they can benefit their children by supporting them as they gain the CBT skills and process the trauma.

A key first step for caregivers is psychoeducation, because often caregivers are unaware that the student's symptoms are related to a traumatic event. The psychoeducation helps put the emotions and behaviors into context and also facilitates more understanding and empathy at home for the student. Second, the caregiver plays a key role in the trauma processing and supporting the in vivo exposure to trauma reminders. Thus, engaging caregivers to help with those processes can make the experiences more manageable for students and ultimately make the intervention components more effective. Finally, Cognitive Behavioral Intervention for Trauma in Schools and Bounce Back both include caregiver informational sessions that describe what is being taught to the students so that caregivers can understand and potentially reinforce the skills as they are acquired.

CONCLUSION

This chapter reviewed some of the key components included in evidence- and school-based interventions related to trauma, including psychoeducation, relaxation, mindfulness, in vivo exposure to trauma reminders, safety planning, development of a trauma narrative, social problem-solving, and caregiver involvement. Resources are available online to learn more about these skills and how they have been applied within school-based interventions, including free online training courses for Cognitive Behavioral Intervention for Trauma in Schools, Support for Students Exposed to Trauma, and Bounce Back. Please see the Resources section for links and additional information.

7

Targeted and Intensive Interventions for Trauma in Schools

As reviewed in Chapter 4, several models have been proposed to enhance school climate and schoolwide supports for students exposed to trauma through the creation of *trauma-informed schools*. Although research on the effectiveness of these models is lacking, the largest area of growth in evidence-based trauma-informed programming for schools has been in the area of interventions for trauma-exposed students. These intervention models have received great interest in part because of their ability to circumvent many of the barriers that impede children from getting mental health care in specialty settings. By delivering mental health care in schools, usually with no cost to the family, many logistical barriers (transportation, scheduling) are removed, and the stigma associated with mental health treatment is decreased as well. To date, the interventions developed specifically for use in schools are targeted intervention programs, designed to help students with elevated symptoms following

http://dx.doi.org/10.1037/0000072-008
Creating Healing School Communities: School-Based Interventions for Students Exposed to Trauma,
by C. D. Santiago, T. Raviv, and L. H. Jaycox
Copyright © 2018 by the American Psychological Association. All rights reserved.

trauma. Students requiring more intensive services are still generally referred out to specialty care, although some evidence-based treatments have been successfully delivered on school campuses. In this chapter, we review each of these in turn.

SCHOOL-BASED TARGETED INTERVENTIONS

Compatible with the Multi-Tiered System of Supports models presented earlier, targeted interventions generally fit into the Tier 2 level. Several interventions have been developed in this area, and some have been evaluated and have demonstrated positive outcomes for students. A comprehensive review of these programs can be found in other sources (Jaycox, Morse, Tanielian, & Stein, 2006; Jaycox, Stein, & Amaya-Jackson, 2008; Jaycox, Stein, Amaya-Jackson, & Morse, 2007; Rolfsnes & Idsoe, 2011). In general, the majority of such interventions involve cognitive behavior therapy (CBT; Rolfsnes & Idsoe, 2011). The core components of CBT that addresses traumatic exposure can be summarized by the acronym PRACTICE: Parenting skills, Psychoeducation, Relaxation skills, Affective Modulation skills, Cognitive coping skills, Trauma narrative, In vivo mastery of trauma reminders, Conjoint sessions for parents, and Enhancing safety (see Exhibit 7.1; Cohen, Mannarino, & Deblinger, 2006). Although

Exhibit 7.1
Evidence-Based Intervention Techniques
■ Parenting skills
■ Psychoeducation
■ Relaxation skills
■ Affective modulation skills
■ Cognitive coping skills
■ Trauma narration
■ In vivo mastery of trauma reminders
■ Conjoint sessions for caregivers
■ Enhancing safety

other techniques and theoretical orientations are also used in some programs (e.g., psychodynamic theories, crisis intervention models), they are less common and tend to be less well-tested to date. One obvious reason for the popularity of CBT in these interventions is its strong evidence base among adults and in different modalities (see Foa, Keane, Friedman, & Cohen, 2008). In addition, these techniques can easily be delivered in group formats in the school setting. For instance, the psychoeducational components of CBT can be delivered in a didactic manner, and the behavioral assignment setting that is integral to CBT is similar to the concept of homework. Table 7.1 summarizes key interventions; we review each in turn in this section. The Resources section of this book lists URLs you can access for more information about these programs.

Table 7.1

Selected School-Based Interventions

Name	Description	Target	Evidence	Dissemination
Cognitive Behavioral Intervention for Trauma in Schools	CBT, 10 group sessions, 1–3 individual sessions, 1 teacher session, 2 parent sessions	5th grade and above	1 RCT, 1 quasi-experimental study, 1 field trial	Wide dissemination through http://www.cbitsprogram.org and national training
Support for Students Exposed to Trauma	CBT, adaptation of CBITS for nonclinical school personnel, 10 group sessions	5th grade and above	1 pilot study	Wide dissemination through http://www.ssetprogram.org and national training
Bounce Back	CBT, adaptation of CBITS for early elementary, 10 group sessions, 2–3 individual sessions	Grades K–5	2 RCTs	Wide dissemination through http://www.bouncebackprogram.org and national training

(continues)

Table 7.1

Selected School-Based Interventions (*Continued*)

Name	Description	Target	Evidence	Dissemination
Trauma-Focused Coping in Schools	CBT, 14 group and 1 individual session	6–18 years	1 quasi-experimental study	Information and training available from developers
Trauma Grief Component Therapy for Adolescents	CBT + grief work, 10–24 50-minute individual or group sessions	12–20 years	1 quasi-experimental study, 3 open trials	Information and training available from developers
Classroom-Based Intervention	CBT, 15 classroom-based sessions	7–19 years	1 RCT	Information and training available from developers
Overshadowing the Threat of Terrorism	CBT for ongoing terrorism context	Grades 2–6	1 RCT	Information and training available from developers
Enhancing Resilience Among Students Experiencing Stress	CBT curriculum for teachers related to ongoing terror-ism context	Grades 3–8	1 RCT, 2 quasi-experimental studies	Information and training available from developers

Note. CBT = cognitive behavior therapy; CBITS = Cognitive Behavioral Intervention for Trauma in Schools; RCT = randomized controlled trial.

Cognitive Behavioral Intervention for Trauma in Schools (CBITS; Jaycox, 2003) is probably the most widely used and accessible program, it has demonstrated improvement in child posttraumatic stress disorder (PTSD) and depressive symptoms in several studies, and it is associated with improved academic outcomes. It involves 10 group sessions, one to three individual sessions, two parent meetings, and one teacher presentation and is delivered by school mental health providers. CBITS is recommended for students in fifth grade or higher. The program was evaluated first in a quasi-experimental study with students who were recent immigrants to Los Angeles and who received the program in Spanish (Kataoka et al., 2003). Results demonstrated a significant decrease in PTSD and depressive symptoms in the group of students who received CBITS as compared with those on a waiting list. A second evaluation among students in the general school population showed similar results in a randomized controlled trial (Stein et al., 2003), with significantly lower scores on measures of depression, PTSD, psychosocial dysfunction among those randomized to receive CBITS, but no difference observed for teacher-reported behavior problems. A subsequent analysis of changes in grades within this study showed that those who received CBITS earlier in the school year had improved grades compared with those who received it later in the year (Kataoka et al., 2011). A field trial in New Orleans following Hurricane Katrina showed comparable results in terms of reductions in PTSD and depression scores among those randomized to CBITS as well as those who received trauma-focused CBT (Jaycox et al., 2010). The program is being implemented broadly within the United States (e.g., New Orleans, Chicago, Los Angeles, San Francisco, several cities in Connecticut).

Three adaptations of CBITS are also promising. Bounce Back is a program that has been developed for younger elementary students. This intervention addresses the same core components but in a more developmentally appropriate manner, and it involves parents to a larger degree than CBITS. It has demonstrated improved child PTSD and anxiety symptoms in one randomized controlled trial (Langley, Gonzalez, Sugar, Solis, & Jaycox, 2015) and improved PTSD symptoms and coping skills in a replication trial (Santiago et al., in press). A second adaptation for CBITS, called Support for Students Exposed to Trauma, was developed for nonclinical school personnel such as teachers or school counselors (Jaycox, Langley, & Dean, 2009). In one pilot study it demonstrated improved outcomes (reductions in PTSD symptoms and depression) and thus is considered a promising approach, even though it led to no changes in parent- or teacher-reported behavior problems (Jaycox, Langley, Stein, et al., 2009). The addition of a family component showed that parent functioning can be improved alongside the child improvements (Santiago, Lennon, Fuller, Brewer, & Kataoka, 2014).

CBITS, Support for Students Exposed to Trauma, and Bounce Back are disseminated through the websites listed in the Resources section of this book, which provide extensive implementation materials and an online training course for each. Live trainings are usually arranged on-site for groups of school mental health providers. Training manuals for Bounce Back and Support for Students Exposed to Trauma are available for download free of charge; the CBITS manual is available for purchase.

Two other school-based interventions have also been evaluated and have demonstrated improved child outcomes: Trauma-Focused Coping in Schools (formerly called Multi-Modality Trauma Treatment; Amaya-Jackson et al., 2003; March et al., 1998), and the Trauma Grief Component Therapy for Adolescents (formerly called the University of California, Los Angeles Trauma/Grief Program; Goenjian et al., 2005; Saltzman, Steinberg, Layne, Aisenberg, & Pynoos, 2001). Both draw on evidence-based practices for trauma, largely cognitive behavior techniques, and have empirical support for the reduction of trauma-related symptoms. Specifically, Trauma-Focused Coping in Schools was evaluated with a staggered start date control design and showed decreases in PTSD, depressive, and anxiety symptoms among 14 treated students (March et al., 1998). These effects were replicated in subsequent studies (Amaya-Jackson et al., 2003). Trauma Grief Component Therapy for Adolescents, targeting community violence in Southern California, showed reductions in PTSD and grief symptoms and improvements in GPA among 26 participants in an open trial, but it did not show changes in depressive symptoms (Layne, Pynoos, & Cardenas, 2001; Saltzman, Pynoos, Layne, Steinberg, & Aisenberg, 2001). A brief version of the program demonstrated reductions in PTSD symptoms in two field trials following an earthquake in Armenia (Goenjian et al., 1997, 2005). In addition, the program was implemented in postwar Bosnia (Layne, Pynoos, Saltzman, et al., 2001), showing greater reductions in PTSD, depression, and maladaptive grief, within the full program as compared with an active comparison condition, with both groups improving significantly (Layne et al., 2008).

Trauma-Focused Coping in Schools is implemented with groups of students, whereas Trauma Grief Component Therapy for Adolescents is run with individual students or in groups. Both of these interventions require 1 to 2 days of in-person training by the program authors. Access to implementation manuals and materials requires contacting the authors of the intervention.

There also have been some notable international efforts in regions affected by disaster or ongoing terrorist threat, five of which have been evaluated. The Classroom-Based Intervention program (Macy, Bary, & Noam, 2003) is a 15-session, classroom-based intervention providing a psychoeducational curriculum for children ages 7 to 19 that is used to address critical needs of children and youth exposed to threat and terror (Macy et al., 2003). A large randomized controlled trial of 664 children and adolescents in Turkey following an earthquake and in the West Bank/ Gaza schools and camps for Palestinian refugees showed improvements among children (ages 4–11) and female adolescents (ages 12–16). Improvements were noted on multiple domains, including communication, social support, negotiation skills, use of relaxation as a coping strategy and, among younger children, decreasing emotional and behavior problems. No improvements were noted among adolescent boys (ages 12–16), however (Khamis, Macy, & Coignez, 2004).

An eight-session program for second through sixth graders called Overshadowing the Threat of Terrorism has been used and evaluated in Israel (Berger, Pat-Horenczyk, & Gelkopf, 2007), showing reduced PTSD, somatic, and anxiety symptoms 2 months after the intervention among children who took part. A related program, more curricular in nature, is Enhancing Resilience Among Students Experiencing Stress (ERASE-S), designed to mitigate the effects of ongoing terrorism. ERASE-S uses teachers to deliver the material and has demonstrated improved outcomes in terms of PTSD and anxiety, as well as reduced stereotypes and discriminatory behaviors (Berger, Gelkopf, & Heineberg, 2012; Berger, Gelkopf, Heineberg, & Zimbardo, 2016; Gelkopf & Berger, 2009). Although these programs use many of the same cognitive behavior techniques as those developed within the United States, none of them have been tested within the United States to date, and their applicability to U.S. schoolchildren is unknown.

OTHER TREATMENTS USED IN SCHOOLS

The interventions described in the preceding section were all developed specifically for use in schools. It is certainly possible to bring clinical services onto school campuses and adapt them to fit the school context and culture. These are typically considered Tier 3 services within the Multi-Tiered System of Supports framework, and a full review of their effectiveness can be found in Foa et al. (2008). Implementing these types of interventions can be challenging as they require more intensive training and supervision for school mental health providers, fitting the sessions into the school day, and handling logistical issues such as space and privacy.

Despite these challenges, these interventions can be good options for students with demonstrated clinical need. We review a few selected interventions here (and summarize the salient points in Table 7.2). For instance, an adaptation of Trauma-Focused Cognitive Behavior Therapy (TF-CBT; Cohen et al., 2006) has begun to be implemented in school settings. Although this treatment has a good deal of empirical support from multiple studies, its effectiveness in schools has not been formally evaluated. Other examples of efforts to bring clinical treatments into schools include Community Outreach Program—Esperanza (De Arellano et al., 2005), which integrates the core components of a TF-CBT package with Parent–Child Interaction Therapy and case management for children ages 4 to 18. Life Skills, Life Stories (Cloitre, Koenen, Cohen, & Han, 2002) is a clinical program for women that was adapted for female high school students with histories of sexual victimization and child abuse. A version for adolescents, called STAIR-A, was tested in schools in a quasi-experimental study and found to reduce depressive symptoms and improve some aspects of functioning (Gudiño, Leonard, & Cloitre, 2016). Trauma Adaptive Recovery Group Education and Therapy for Adolescents (Ford, Mahoney, & Russo, 2001) focuses on body self-regulation, memory, interpersonal problem solving, and stress management for youths ages 10 to 18 affected by physical or sexual abuse, domestic or community violence, or traumatic loss. Structured Psychotherapy for Adolescents Responding to Chronic Stress (DeRosa & Pelcovitz, 2009) for teens (ages 12–19) exposed to chronic interpersonal traumas combines CBT and dialectical behavior therapy approaches (including mindfulness) to improve coping, affect regulation, relationships, and functioning in the present. Although each of these treatments has some evidence of their effectiveness, their use in schools has not been formally tested.

Table 7.2

Selected Clinical Treatments Used in School Settings

Name	Description	Target	Application in schools
Trauma-Focused Cognitive Behavior Therapy (Jaycox et al., 2010)	Cognitive behavior therapy in parent–child dyads	Ages 3–18	Limited use in schools, not formally tested
Community Outreach Program— Esperanza (De Arellano et al., 2005)	Trauma-Focused Cognitive Behavior Therapy components plus Parent–Child Interaction Therapy components and case management for parent–child dyads, delivered in homes and community settings	Ages 4–18	Designed for use in schools and other community settings
Life Skills, Life Stories (Gudiño, Leonard, & Cloitre, 2016)	Group sessions to build social emotional competencies	Girls, ages 12–21 with a history of abuse	Some use in schools, tested in one study with good effects
Trauma Adaptive Recovery Group Education and Therapy for Adolescents (Ford, Mahoney, & Russo, 2001)	Group or individual cognitive behavior therapy with focus on emotion regulation	Ages 10–18, complex trauma	Designed for use in juvenile justice settings (community or residential) or schools
Structured Psychotherapy for Adolescents Responding to Chronic Stress (DeRosa & Pelcovitz, 2009)	Group cognitive behavior therapy and dialectical behavior therapy elements	Ages 12–19, complex trauma	Designed for use in clinical settings, not formally tested in schools

CONCLUSION

This chapter summarized the most widely known and evaluated school-based programs for trauma. However, many more programs have been developed locally to respond to disasters, school crises such as shootings, and the everyday occurrence of family and community violence. These local efforts often remain untested, and so their effectiveness is unknown. The few programs examined in randomized controlled trials show moderate to large improvements in child outcomes (Jaycox, Stein, & Amaya-Jackson, 2008). School mental health providers together with their school administration can select programs that will best fit their school environment and student body. Programs that have been designed for and tested within schools, with good evidence, will likely be most successful.

8

Special Considerations for Implementing Interventions in Schools

Implementing services to support mental health and social–emotional adjustment in schools is not without challenges, ranging from concrete barriers to organizational impediments and legal considerations. This chapter is intended to highlight some of the common considerations and challenges faced by school mental health providers and provide guidance and strategies for overcoming them. In particular, this chapter discusses issues related to informed consent, privacy and confidentiality within a school setting, working with teachers and caregivers, and the importance of self-care in the context of secondary traumatic stress. It concludes with recommendations for improving the sustainability of trauma-based services in schools.

http://dx.doi.org/10.1037/0000072-009
Creating Healing School Communities: School-Based Interventions for Students Exposed to Trauma, by C. D. Santiago, T. Raviv, and L. H. Jaycox
Copyright © 2018 by the American Psychological Association. All rights reserved.

CONSENT FOR SCHOOL-BASED SERVICES

When implementing a Tier 2 or Tier 3 mental health intervention, active consent from a legal guardian is typically required. Still, school policies differ in this regard; some require active written consent, whereas other schools provide a notice of assignment to school interventions or programs that only require caregivers to opt out if they do not want their child to participate. Thus, it is important to check with school administrators if you are not familiar with your school's policy. In any case, reaching out to caregivers for consent can be an opportunity to engage them in treatment and form an initial collaborative relationship. We describe strategies for engaging caregivers in a later section in this chapter.

Several considerations are key when obtaining informed consent (see Exhibit 8.1). In general, school mental health providers should be prepared to describe the intervention, to discuss confidentiality and limits to confidentiality, and to share any expectations for caregiver involvement. In terms of explaining consent and intervention information, it is essential to use language and terms easily understood by caregivers (American Psychological Association, 2017). Thus, school mental health providers should strive for jargon-free explanations of the intervention and provide

---

Exhibit 8.1

Considerations for Informed Consent

√ Be familiar with your school's policy
√ Describe the intervention
√ Give examples of program components
√ Use easily understandable language
√ Use consent as an opportunity to engage caregivers in treatment
√ Discuss confidentiality
√ Review limits to confidentiality
√ Ensure accurate translations for non–English-speaking families
√ Obtain assent from student

easy-to-understand information about the scope of and limits to confidentiality. Furthermore, they should provide examples of the kinds of approaches and skills in which students will be engaged. Checking in with caregivers at several points about questions or concerns can facilitate greater communication and understanding during the consent process. Ensuring that consent documents are accurately translated is also important for caregivers who do not speak English fluently.

In addition to ensuring that caregivers understand the program and provide consent, it is important to obtain assent (verbal or written) from students themselves. School mental health providers should explain the program in age-appropriate language and ask students if they are willing to participate. Explaining confidentiality and its limits to students is another important part of obtaining assent. Confidentiality can be a particular concern for some students in the school setting. It is important to explain that while teachers and other students may know that they are participating in an intervention for trauma, specifics of their situation will not be shared with other individuals except when mandated reporting is required. Some students may be unsure whether they want to participate, and they should be given the option to participate as a "trial run" and to discontinue the intervention if they choose to do so after a few sessions (e.g., Gola et al., 2016).

Obtaining consent from caregivers can be an opportunity to engage caregivers in the program, but it can also be challenging. Logistical barriers may arise if caregivers are difficult to reach in person or by phone; other barriers may be related to stigma, confidentiality concerns, and understanding of the program. Sending letters home and maintaining phone contact are key for working caregivers who may be unavailable to meet during the day. Furthermore, meeting caregivers at drop-off or pick-up times or visiting the home are other strategies that have been successful for engaging caregivers in the consent process. In a qualitative study of an early elementary intervention, caregivers suggested that the process of obtaining informed consent should include several components, including information being sent home as well as the opportunity to speak or meet privately to dispel concerns and reduce stigma (Langley, Santiago,

Rodríguez, & Zelaya, 2013). Thus, school mental health providers who contact caregivers for consent might offer to send additional information about the program home and offer to discuss the program in person or by phone. Caregivers in the study by Langley, Santiago, et al. (2013) noted the need to be clear about limits to confidentiality but also wanted assurances that school mental health records are separate from school academic records. Privacy and confidentiality are discussed in more detail in the next section.

PRIVACY AND CONFIDENTIALITY WITHIN A SCHOOL CONTEXT

All mental health providers are trained on the ethical and legal requirements regarding privacy and confidentiality. However, the school setting is a unique context in which to provide mental health services, and there is often confusion about how to maintain privacy and confidentiality within schools because regulations, policies, and procedures might not be consistent, and assumptions and expectations might not be verbalized. To add to the confusion, mental health providers in schools may be employees of the school or may be employed by community mental health agencies; services may be provided by a licensed clinician, unlicensed clinician, or graduate student intern; and services may be funded by the school, by a grant, or may be paid for through billing of Medicaid or insurance. Each of these circumstances carries with it separate requirements regarding documentation, communication, informed consent, and confidentiality so that two individuals providing the same services within the same school may be governed by different rules.

Two sets of federal guidelines often operate simultaneously within schools: the Family Educational Rights and Privacy Act (FERPA; 1974) and the Health Insurance Portability and Accountability Act (HIPAA; 1996). FERPA and HIPAA set different standards related to confidentiality and information exchange (Weist & Paternite, 2006). FERPA applies to all personnel employed by the school and states that student records may be accessed by family and relevant school employees but may not be shared with agencies outside the school district without consent (Weist et al., 2012). FERPA guidelines allow for relatively open communication among school personnel regarding children who have received trauma treatment and how symptoms may be affecting school performance. However, FERPA guidelines do not define mental health providers who are employed by a community mental health agency as school personnel, and thus signed release forms may be required before schools can provide pertinent information about a child's individualized education program or other school metrics to community mental health providers, even if they are providing services in the school. Community mental health providers who offer services in school may be bound by HIPAA guidelines, especially if services are being billed to health insurance companies. HIPAA regulations require a guardian to sign a release before sharing any mental health information. This may contribute to tensions in the school setting because educators and school personnel are typically accustomed to the more open communication allowed under FERPA (Weist & Paternite, 2006; Weist et al., 2012).

It is recommended that mental health providers in schools acquaint themselves with the formal guidelines of FERPA and HIPAA, the ethical standards of their profession (e.g., National Association of School Psychologists Ethics Code or National Association of Social Workers Standards for School Social Work Services), and state and district guidelines to determine guidelines for information sharing (Perfect & Morris, 2011). In all cases, the rights of the client and family should be paramount, with information shared only as necessary to support students' educational programming and socialization at school and to ensure safety of students and staff. Confidentiality and limits of confidentiality must be discussed openly with students and families at the outset of services. When students participate in a group intervention, it is important to establish group norms that include an expectation that the information provided by other group members will remain private. For students affected by trauma, it is particularly important to discuss mandated reporting of abuse or neglect because these topics come up in the course of trauma therapy and may be the reason for referral. Likewise, it is essential to work with school personnel on developing a plan to handle these instances that is compatible with school norms and procedures and complies with mandated reporting guidelines.

COLLABORATION WITH TEACHERS

As discussed in Chapter 5, it is important to partner with teachers prior to implementing a Tier 2 trauma-focused intervention. However, it is also critical to continue this partnership during the actual implementation. A key recommendation for sustaining teacher support and collaboration is to maintain ongoing communication with teachers (Baweja et al., 2016; Langley, Santiago, et al., 2013). School mental health providers may need to explain the limits that confidentiality places on this communication, as reviewed in the preceding section. However, informing teachers about the skills that are being developed in intervention sessions each week puts teachers in a position to support such skills in the classroom. Weekly notes or e-mails about the focus of each intervention session may help teachers feel included in supporting students who participate in the intervention and help students generalize skills learned in the intervention to the classroom setting. For example, if teachers know that relaxation strategies were learned in the last session, they may be able to prompt or support a student's use of relaxation should they become distressed in the classroom. School mental health providers may also want to share psychoeducation about secondary trauma so that teachers working with traumatized students can practice good self-care as well. In addition, sharing aggregated outcome data (e.g., symptom reduction, improvements in skills, changes in attendance, discipline, or grades) can also help sustain support for school-based interventions. Thus, school mental health providers may wish to share these improvements with teachers individually or offer a brief presentation summarizing aggregated improvement among students who received a Tier 2 trauma-focused intervention during a staff meeting. Finally, collaborating with teachers and students to identify ways in which students will make up assignments they may have missed can also reduce both teacher and student frustration.

ENGAGING PARENTS AND CAREGIVERS
IN TREATMENT

Caregiver involvement is a key component of school-based trauma-focused interventions, but it remains a challenge for many school mental health providers. For example, one study suggests that caregiver participation in Cognitive Behavioral Intervention for Trauma in Schools (CBITS) has been fairly low, with only 37% of caregivers attending at least one of the two recommended psychoeducation sessions (Kataoka et al., 2003). For younger students, caregiver involvement may be even more critical as parental support has been identified as a critical component of evidence-based care for young children who have experienced trauma (Cohen & Mannarino, 2008). In a trial evaluating the early elementary intervention Bounce Back, 97% of caregivers attended at least one joint session with the child and school mental health provider (Langley et al., 2015). This level of involvement was found in the context of a research-supported trial of Bounce Back, but it suggests that a high level of caregiver involvement can be achieved, especially for younger students.

A number of barriers can complicate adult involvement in school-based programming. Single-parent status, low socioeconomic status, parent psychopathology, ethnic minority status, and neighborhood disadvantage have all been identified as factors related to lower rates of parental or caregiver engagement in clinical services (Nock & Ferriter, 2005; Snell-Johns, Mendez, & Smith, 2004). Caregivers report barriers such as limited time, scheduling conflicts, and lack of transportation and child care (Davis, Ressler, Schwartz, Stephens, & Bradley, 2008; Stevens, Kelleher, Ward-Estes, & Hayes, 2006). Furthermore, when caregivers perceive little benefit to services, do not view the treatment goals as relevant, or view providers as judgmental or lacking empathy, they are less likely to remain engaged in their child's treatment (Gross, Julion, & Fogg, 2001). In addition, caregivers may feel guilt about their child's trauma or have their own trauma (Lieberman et al., 2005), which can prevent full engagement in child treatment for trauma. Despite the challenges to successfully involving caregivers in treatment, recent research suggests that many caregivers would like to be more involved in their child's school-based treatment (Santiago et al., 2015). Some caregivers suggested additional sessions and more contact with school mental health providers so that they could better support their children in using skills and recovering from trauma. Thus, it is critical for school mental health providers to not assume that caregivers are uninterested or unavailable to participate in school-based interventions for trauma. Even in cases where the caregiver has been involved in the trauma in some way (e.g., domestic violence), caregivers are often still open to participation when approached with nonstigmatizing language and when safety has been established.

Creative efforts may be needed to accommodate working caregivers as well as those facing challenges associated with poverty or their own mental health symptoms. Caregiver involvement may be especially important for students with more severe symptoms (Santiago, Lennon, Fuller, Brewer, & Kataoka, 2014). McKay and Bannon (2004) addressed the importance of providing intensive engagement interventions during initial contacts with families to prevent caregiver dropout. Using telephone engagement strategies resulted in a 30% increase in initial appointments kept among urban low-income families (McKay, McCadam, & Gonzales, 1996). Key components of engagement interventions such as addressing logistical barriers and exploring ambivalence about participating in services are important for overcoming barriers to participation among low-income families. In addition, community partners have emphasized the importance of presenting programs using jargon-free and destigmatizing language— for example, describing the program's focus on skill building for managing stress rather than focusing on trauma or deficits (Santiago et al., 2014). Additionally, asking caregivers about their goals and hopes for their child can help school mental health providers focus engagement efforts. Caregivers who value academics may benefit from hearing about how an intervention might improve academic engagement and functioning, whereas other caregivers may benefit from hearing about how caregiver sessions may give them tools to support better communication and trust with their child. In any case, establishing a partnership with caregivers in reaching mutual goals is key during initial contacts with families. In previous research, schools with the highest level of caregiver involvement in CBITS reported consistent and extensive outreach as well as a strong belief

---

Exhibit 8.2

Key Caregiver Engagement Strategies

- Use nonstigmatizing language.
- Problem solve logistical barriers together.
- Offer phone or in-person meetings and use multiple methods of communication depending on preferences (phone, in-person, letters, e-mail).
- Ask caregivers about their goals for their child and discuss how the intervention can be consistent.
- Ask caregivers about their questions, concerns, or doubts.

---

that caregiver engagement was essential to the intervention (Santiago et al., 2015). A summary of key engagement strategies is provided in Exhibit 8.2.

Still, it is important to recognize that school mental health providers have tremendous demands on their time, making extensive outreach difficult. Furthermore, symptom improvement has been demonstrated with school-based interventions (e.g., CBITS) even with limited caregiver involvement (Stein et al., 2003). Preimplementation strategies for facilitating strong school–caregiver relationships, as described in Chapter 5, can facilitate engagement during treatment. School mental health providers with cofacilitators may find it helpful to share the caregiver engagement work so that it is less burdensome.

SECONDARY TRAUMATIC STRESS

Working with students exposed to trauma is often an extremely rewarding experience, but listening to children's trauma stories can also affect mental health providers' own emotional well-being. The National Child Traumatic Stress Network (NCTSN) defines *secondary traumatic stress* as the emotional distress associated with hearing about the trauma experiences of another person (NCTSN, Secondary Traumatic Stress Committee, 2016). Symptoms of secondary traumatic distress can mirror those of posttraumatic stress disorder (NCTSN, Secondary Traumatic Stress Committee, 2011, 2016; Van Dernoot Lipsky, 2009; see Exhibit 8.3). These symptoms not only affect ongoing intervention work with students but also diminish healthy functioning and quality of life. Thus, it is important to take steps to prevent secondary traumatic stress, to regularly assess for symptoms of secondary traumatic stress, and get support to address these symptoms if they arise.

When considering prevention of secondary traumatic stress, school-based mental health providers should (a) familiarize themselves with signs and symptoms of secondary traumatic stress, (b) use supervision to process reactions to trauma-based work, and (c) use self-care strategies. If school mental health providers have access to regular supervision, exploring reactions to trauma interventions is essential. Supervision can be a safe space in which to process emotional reactions to hearing about students' trauma and get support from supervisors with trauma intervention experience. School mental health providers may also be able to process their reactions with cofacilitators or other providers within their school or district; these colleagues provide an opportunity for a self-care accountability "buddy" system, in which the buddy checks in with a provider on his or her practice and commitment to self-care. Effective self-care strategies can range from

---

Exhibit 8.3

Common Symptoms of Secondary Traumatic Stress

- Difficulty listening to clients
- Increased arousal
- Sleeplessness
- Chronic exhaustion
- Hopelessness
- Anger or cynicism
- Fear
- Guilt
- Disruptions in perceptions of safety and trust

physical self-care (e.g., good nutrition, exercise), psychological self-care (e.g., time for self-reflection, engaging in one's own therapy), emotional self-care (e.g., spending time with friends or family), spiritual self-care (e.g., meditate, reflect, pray), and professional self-care (e.g., getting supervision or consultation, taking lunch breaks; Saakvitne, Pearlman, & Staff of TSI/CAAP, 1996). An overview and assessment of self-care strategies is available online (see Resources #28 and #29 in the Resources section at the end of this book; NCTSN, Secondary Traumatic Stress Committee, 2011; Saakvitne et al., 1996).

When secondary traumatic stress symptoms are not manageable even with good self-care strategies, it is important to seek additional support. This may include engaging in therapy: Cognitive behavioral and mindfulness interventions offer the best support for helping with secondary traumatic stress (NCTSN, Secondary Traumatic Stress Committee, 2011). Additional strategies may involve adjusting one's caseload, shifting work responsibilities to allow for a break from trauma intervention, and/or taking time off from work.

SUSTAINABILITY

In Chapter 5, several preimplementation strategies are offered that can support successful implementation and sustainability of Tier 2 interventions within schools. However, school mental health providers often face additional challenges that threaten the sustainability of continued implementation of Tier 2 interventions year to year. In one study examining implementation of CBITS, competing responsibilities were identified as the top challenge by nonimplementers and the second highest challenge for those providers that did implement CBITS (Langley et al., 2010). School mental health providers have multiple demands on their time and a number of competing responsibilities and priorities within their schools. When possible, partnerships between school-employed and community-employed mental health providers working on the same school campuses can minimize the time demands. In general, community-employed providers reported fewer competing demands on the school's campus, allowing for more time to prepare materials for group, whereas school-employed providers were better able to help set up the logistics of space and scheduling as school employees (Langley et al., 2010). Even when these types of school–community partnerships are not possible, it may be possible to cofacilitate Tier 2 interventions with other school-based mental health providers to decrease burden. Partnering with educators and support staff for help with referrals, preparation of materials, and logistics can also decrease burden. Even if they are not within your school, contact with other providers implementing Tier 2 interventions within the district or region can also facilitate sharing of strategies and provision of support. For school mental health providers who still find themselves without adequate support, the online community of providers implementing school-based interventions is growing. For example, the CBITS website offers forums where providers can post questions, strategies, and tools to aid in implementation and sustainability.

In addition to competing responsibilities, school mental health providers are often faced with changing policies, priorities, or initiatives within schools as well as scarce resources to support mental health interventions. Laying the groundwork with administrators and teachers as described in Chapter 5 to increase support and buy-in is essential; continuing this line of communication over time is also important. For example, at the start of each school year, it may be helpful to share information about the Tier 2 interventions that were implemented in the prior year, how many students were served, and any indicators of benefit or improvement from the interventions (e.g., symptom improvement, academic improvement) to reengage educators to support the work. This type of work can also help when logistical challenges are encountered, because educators may be more open to solving space difficulties or challenges associated with missed class time when they are aware that the intervention is helping students year to year. Changes in or lack of funding can be another barrier that is typically out of the control of school mental health providers. As described in Chapter 5, creative solutions to funding shortages typically involve using multiple sources of funding, federal grants, state funding, fee-for-service reimbursements through private or public insurance, and solicited funds from private donors or foundations (S. W. Evans et al., 2003).

CONCLUSION

There are several special considerations for implementing trauma interventions in schools. School mental health providers often need to take extra steps to engage caregivers in the consent and treatment process, which can differ from a setting where parents are bringing their child to a clinic for treatment. Furthermore, school mental health providers should familiarize themselves with relevant policies such as FERPA and HIPAA. Using strategies to collaborate and partner with educators and caregivers can facilitate treatment for the student and sustainability of the program long-term. Finally, school mental health providers must also ensure that they are engaging in good self-care while providing support for students exposed to trauma. Being aware of secondary traumatic stress and taking steps to prevent it are essential for school mental health providers to continue the important work they do to support students.

Conclusion

Rates of trauma exposure among children indicate that traumatic experiences are very common. Trauma exposure among children is linked to posttraumatic stress disorder, anxiety, depression, poor school functioning, decreased rates of high school graduation, and aggressive and delinquent behavior (Costello et al., 2002; Lynch, 2003; Overstreet & Mathews, 2011). Although children are resilient, some students need intervention to reduce distress and support healthy functioning. Thus, it is critical for school mental health providers to consider trauma exposure when working with students.

Children spend a substantial portion of their time in schools. Schools can serve as a nonstigmatizing entry point for treatment and reduce barriers to accessing care. Both the social–emotional learning movement and the Multi-Tiered System of Supports model provide frameworks for understanding the various aspects of trauma-related interventions available to schools. Interventions at different tiers can improve social–emotional functioning as well as academic performance, absences, and behavior. Creating trauma-informed schools will help to identify and address students' mental health needs, supporting their learning and development.

http://dx.doi.org/10.1037/0000072-010
Creating Healing School Communities: School-Based Interventions for Students Exposed to Trauma,
by C. D. Santiago, T. Raviv, and L. H. Jaycox
Copyright © 2018 by the American Psychological Association. All rights reserved.

Efforts to educate teachers and administrators about the impact of trauma on students, implement universal interventions that build students' social–emotional learning skills, plan for managing school crises, and create collaborative relationships with families and community partners help to create a healing school community.

In addition to these universal interventions, offering targeted school-based intervention for trauma is also critical for creating a healing school community. School mental health providers should consider several important elements prior to implementing a school-based intervention for trauma. They should establish collaborative partnerships with administrators, teachers, and caregivers. Considering school context, providers can select the best screening strategy for their school. Careful selection and administration of screening measures will also support evidence-based tracking of student outcomes (e.g., pre- to post-intervention comparison).

Chapter 7 presents several programs, including Cognitive-Behavioral Intervention for Trauma in Schools (CBITS; Jaycox, 2003), the most widely evidence-based and accessible program. CBITS includes 10 group sessions that foster understanding and normalization of trauma reactions and promote skills to manage and improve trauma symptoms (e.g., relaxation, cognitive coping skills, social problem solving). CBITS also includes one to three individual sessions focused on a trauma narrative, as well as two parent meetings and one teacher presentation. CBITS is recommended for students in fifth grade or higher. Bounce Back (Langley, Gonzalez, Sugar, Solis, & Jaycox, 2015), a program that was developed for younger elementary students, is a promising adaptation of CBITS. Bounce Back includes similar core components as CBITS, but it has been adapted to be more developmentally appropriate for younger children. CBITS and other evidence-based programs typically take a cognitive behavioral approach. Key components of such approaches can be summarized by the acronym PRACTICE: Parenting skills, Psychoeducation, Relaxation skills, Affective Modulation skills, Cognitive coping skills, Trauma narrative, In vivo mastery of trauma reminders, Conjoint sessions for parents, and Enhancing safety (Cohen,

Mannarino, & Deblinger, 2006), although the different elements vary across the specific interventions.

When implementing trauma interventions in schools, there are several common considerations and challenges. For example, extra efforts to engage caregivers in the consent and treatment process are often needed for school-based services. Partnering with educators and caregivers can help to overcome barriers to a program's implementation and promote its long-term sustainability. School mental health providers should take steps to prioritize good self-care while providing trauma interventions. Preventing and managing secondary traumatic stress is critical for school mental health providers to continue supporting students exposed to trauma.

FUTURE DIRECTIONS

This book provides a summary of the best available treatments for trauma in schools. More evaluations of school-based trauma interventions are needed to establish key treatments as effective for reducing symptoms and promoting school functioning. In addition to evaluating interventions, research on the implementation of these interventions in schools is also needed. While several studies have identified key barriers and facilitators to the implementation of school-based interventions for trauma (e.g., Langley, Nadeem, Kataoka, Stein, & Jaycox, 2010), more work is needed to identify the best strategies for ensuring that interventions are implemented successfully with adequate support, training, and supervision throughout the process.

IMPLICATIONS FOR SCHOOL MENTAL HEALTH PROVIDERS

We hope this book will guide school mental health providers in their efforts to raise awareness of trauma, support students exposed to trauma through trauma-sensitive schools, and implement targeted interventions for students with elevated symptoms. Exhibit 1 summarizes key

---

Exhibit 1

Key Components of Evidence-Based Practice for Trauma in Schools

1. Use the Multi-Tiered System of Supports framework to guide intervention efforts with students (see Chapter 3).
2. Share psychoeducation material about trauma with educators to increase schoolwide trauma-sensitive programs and establish partnerships for targeted interventions (see Chapters 4 and 5).
3. Use a standardized measure of posttraumatic stress disorder symptoms for screening and progress monitoring (see Chapter 5).
4. Use evidence-based components (e.g., PRACTICE: Parenting skills, Psychoeducation, Relaxation skills, Affective Modulation skills, Cognitive coping skills, Trauma narrative, In vivo mastery of trauma reminders, Conjoint sessions for parents, and Enhancing safety; see Chapters 6 and 7) in individual work with students exposed to trauma.
5. Implement programs with a strong evidence base (e.g., Cognitive Behavioral Intervention for Trauma in Schools; see Chapter 7).
6. Make extra efforts to engage caregivers in treatment efforts (see Chapter 8).
7. Practice good self-care (see Chapter 8).

---

considerations for school mental health providers who work in supporting students exposed to trauma.

School mental health providers play a critical role in supporting students who have experienced trauma. We hope this book is a resource for them as they continue this important work.

Resources

PROMOTING TRAUMA-INFORMED SCHOOLS

1. Substance Abuse and Mental Health Services Administration's Trauma Informed Approach: https://www.samhsa.gov/nctic/trauma-interventions
2. Trauma and Learning Policy Initiative: http://www.traumasensitiveschools.org
3. National Child Traumatic Stress Network: http://www.nctsn.org
4. Treatment and Services Adaptation Center for Resiliency, Hope, and Wellness in Schools: https://traumaawareschools.org
5. Department of Education, Crisis Planning: http://www2.ed.gov/admins/lead/safety/emergencyplan/crisisplanning.pdf
6. Positive Behavioral Interventions and Supports: http://www.pbis.org
7. Collaborative for Academic, Social, and Emotional Learning: http://www.casel.org
8. Center for School Mental Health at the University of Maryland: https://csmh.umaryland.edu
9. Psychological First Aid Manual: http://www.nctsn.org/content/psychological-first-aid-schoolspfa

INCREASING AWARENESS OF TRAUMA
FOR EDUCATORS

10. Seven Slide Series: http://childtrauma.org/cta-library/brain-dev-neuroscience/
11. Making Caring Common Project at the Harvard Graduate School of Education: http://mcc.gse.harvard.edu/files/gse-mcc/files/relationship_mapping_pitch_and_guide_0_0.pdf?m=1448056924
12. "Students and Trauma" DVD: http://www.nctsn.org/sites/default/files/assets/pdfs/students_and_trauma_dvd_orderform.pdf
13. Listen, Protect, Connect—Model & Teach: Psychological First Aid (PFA) for Students and Teachers: https://www.ready.gov/sites/default/files/documents/files/PFA_SchoolCrisis.pdf
14. National Child Traumatic Stress Network Trauma Toolkit for Educators (2008): http://www.nctsn.org/resources/audiences/school-personnel/trauma-toolkit

INTERVENTION APPLICATIONS

15. Relaxation App: http://t2health.dcoe.mil/apps/breathe2relax
16. Mindfulness App: http://www.mindyeti.com
17. Trauma-Focused Cognitive Behavior Therapy Triangle of Life App: https://tfcbt.org/tf-cbt-triangle-of-life/

SCHOOL-BASED TREATMENTS

18. Cognitive-Behavioral Intervention for Trauma in Schools: http://www.cbitsprogram.org
19. Bounce Back: http://www.bouncebackprogram.org
20. Support for Students Exposed to Trauma: http://www.ssetprogram.org
21. Trauma-Focused Coping in Schools: http://www.nctsn.org/sites/default/files/assets/pdfs/mmtt_general.pdf
22. Trauma Grief Component Therapy for Adolescents: http://www.nctsnet.org/nctsn_assets/pdfs/promising_practices/TGCT_fact_sheet_%203-22-07.pdf

ADDITIONAL TREATMENTS USED
IN SCHOOL SETTINGS

23. Trauma-Focused Cognitive Behavioral Therapy: http://www.nctsn. org/nctsn_assets/pdfs/promising_practices/TF-CBT_fact_sheet_ 3-20-07.pdf

24. Community Outreach Program—Esperanza: http://www.nctsnet.org/ nctsn_assets/pdfs/materials_for_applicants/COPE_2-11-05.pdf

25. Life Skills, Life Stories: http://www.nctsnet.org/nctsn_assets/pdfs/ promising_practices/Life_Skills_Life_Stories_10-24-06.pdf

26. Trauma Adaptive Recovery Group Education and Therapy for Adolescents and Pre-Adolescents Model Program: http://www.nctsnet. org/nctsn_assets/pdfs/materials_for_applicants/TARGET_2-11-05

27. Structured Psychotherapy for Adolescents Responding to Chronic Stress: http://www.nctsnet.org/nctsn_assets/pdfs/promising_practices/ SPARCS_General.pdf

SELF-CARE RESOURCES

28. National Child Traumatic Stress Network, Secondary Traumatic Stress: A fact sheet for child-serving professionals: http://www.nctsn.org/ resources/topics/secondary-traumatic-stress

29. Overview and assessment of self-care strategies: http://www.creating- joy.com/taskforce/PDF/ACA_taskforce_assessment.pdf

ADDITIONAL RESOURCES

30. National Child Traumatic Stress Network Reading Lists: http://www. nctsn.org/resources/online-research/reading-lists

31. Technical Assistance Partnership for Child and Family Mental Health: http://www.air.org/sites/default/files/downloads/report/ Sustaining%20School%20Mental%20Health%20Programs_4.pdf

32. National Child Traumatic Stress Network Measures Database: http:// www.nctsn.org/resources/online-research/measures-review

References

Allegheny Health Network. (2015). *TF-CBT Triangle of Life* [Mobile application software]. Retrieved from https://play.google.com/store/apps/details?id=com. AHN.ETC.TriangleOfLife&hl=en

Allensworth, D., Lawson, E., Nicholson, L., & Wyche, J. (1997). *Schools and health: Our nation's investment.* Washington, DC: National Academy Press.

Amaya-Jackson, L., Reynolds, V., Murray, M. C., McCarthy, G., Nelson, A., Cherney, M. S., . . . March, J. S. (2003). Cognitive-behavioral treatment for pediatric posttraumatic stress disorder: Protocol and application in school and community settings. *Cognitive and Behavioral Practice, 10,* 204–213. http:// dx.doi.org/10.1016/S1077-7229(03)80032-9

American Psychiatric Association. (2013). *Diagnostical and statistical manual of mental disorders* (5th ed.). Arlington, VA: Author.

American Psychological Association. (2017). *Ethical principles of psychologists and code of conduct* (2002, Amended June 1, 2010 and January 1, 2017). Retrieved from http://www.apa.org/ethics/code/index.aspx

American Psychological Association. (n.d.). *Ethnic and racial minorities & socio-economic status.* Retrieved from http://www.apa.org/pi/ses/resources/publica-tions/factsheet-erm.aspx

Americans With Disabilities Act of 1990, Pub. L. No. 101-336, ¶ 2, 104 Stat. 328 (1991).

Baweja, S., Santiago, C. D., Vona, P., Pears, G., Langley, A., & Kataoka, S. (2016). Improving implementation of a school-based program for traumatized students: Identifying factors that promote teacher support and collaboration. *School Mental Health, 8,* 120–131. http://dx.doi.org/10.1007/s12310-015-9170-z

Bell, C. C., & Jenkins, E. J. (1993). Community violence and children on Chicago's southside. *Psychiatry: Interpersonal and Biological Processes, 56,* 46–54. http:// dx.doi.org/10.1080/00332747.1993.11024620

Berger, R., Gelkopf, M., & Heineberg, Y. (2012). A teacher-delivered intervention for adolescents exposed to ongoing and intense traumatic war-related stress: A quasi-randomized controlled study. *Journal of Adolescent Health, 51*, 453–461. http://dx.doi.org/10.1016/j.jadohealth.2012.02.011

Berger, R., Gelkopf, M., Heineberg, Y., & Zimbardo, P. (2016). A school-based intervention for reducing posttraumatic symptomatology and intolerance during political violence. *Journal of Educational Psychology, 108*, 761–771. http://dx.doi.org/10.1002/jts.20225

Berger, R., Pat-Horenczyk, R., & Gelkopf, M. (2007). School-based intervention for prevention and treatment of elementary-students' terror-related distress in Israel: A quasi-randomized controlled trial. *Journal of Traumatic Stress, 20*, 541–551. http://dx.doi.org/10.1002/jts.20225

Bethell, C. D., Newacheck, P., Hawes, E., & Halfon, N. (2014). Adverse childhood experiences: Assessing the impact on health and school engagement and the mitigating role of resilience. *Health Affairs, 33*, 2106–2115. http://dx.doi.org/10.1377/hlthaff.2014.0914

Bradshaw, C. P., Waasdorp, T. E., & Leaf, P. J. (2012). Effects of school-wide positive behavioral interventions and supports on child behavior problems. *Pediatrics, 130*, e1136–e1145. http://dx.doi.org/10.1542/peds.2012-0243

Breslau, N., Davis, G. C., Andreski, P., & Peterson, E. (1991). Traumatic events and posttraumatic stress disorder in an urban population of young adults. *Archives of General Psychiatry, 48*(3), 216–222. http://dx.doi.org/10.1001/archpsyc.1991.01810270028003

Brymer, M., Jacobs, A., Layne, C., Pynoos, R., Ruzek, J., Steinberg, A., . . . Watson, P. (2012). *Psychological first aid for schools: Field operations guide* (2nd ed.). Los Angeles, CA: National Child Traumatic Stress Network.

The Center for Health and Healthcare in Schools. (2012). *Children's mental health needs, disparities, and school-based services: A fact sheet.* Retrieved from http://www.healthinschools.org/issue-areas/school-based-mental-health/background/fact-sheet/#sthash.XqrHQ7hu.dpbs

Chafouleas, S. M., Johnson, A. H., Overstreet, S., & Santos, N. M. (2016). Toward a blueprint for trauma-informed service delivery in schools. *School Mental Health, 8*, 144–162. http://dx.doi.org/10.1007/s12310-015-9166-8

Chan, Y. C., & Yeung, J. W. (2009). Children living with violence within the family and its sequel: A meta-analyst from 1995–2006. *Aggression and Violent Behavior, 14*, 313–322. http://dx.doi.org/10.1016/j.avb.2009.04.001

Children's Mental Health Act of 2003, 405 ILCS 49.

Child Trends. (2014). *Immigrant children.* Retrieved from https://www.childtrends.org/?indicators=immigrant-children

Cloitre, M., Koenen, K. C., Cohen, L. R., & Han, H. (2002). Skills training in affective and interpersonal regulation followed by exposure: A phase-based treatment for PTSD related to childhood abuse. *Journal of Consulting and Clinical Psychology, 70*, 1067–1074. http://dx.doi.org/10.1037/0022-006X.70.5.1067

Cloitre, M., Stolbach, B. C., Herman, J. L., van der Kolk, B., Pynoos, R., Wang, J., & Petkova, E. (2009). A developmental approach to complex PTSD: Childhood and adult cumulative trauma as predictors of symptom complexity. *Journal of Traumatic Stress, 22*, 399–408. http://dx.doi.org/10.1002/jts.20444

Cohen, J. A., & Mannarino, A. P. (2008). Trauma-focused cognitive behavioral therapy for children and parents. *Child and Adolescent Mental Health, 13*, 158–162. http://dx.doi.org/10.1111/j.1475-3588.2008.00502.x

Cohen, J. A., Mannarino, A. P., & Deblinger, E. (2006). *Treating trauma and traumatic grief in children and adolescents*. New York, NY: Guilford Press.

Cole, S. F., Eisner, A., Gregory, M., & Ristuccia, J. (2013). *Creating and advocating for trauma-sensitive schools*. Massachusetts Advocates for Children. Retrieved from http://www.traumasensitiveschools.org

Collaborative for Academic, Social, and Emotional Learning. (2016). *Policy recommendations to sustain SEL*. Retrieved from http://www.casel.org/policy/recommendations/

Colorado Department of Education. (2016). *Colorado multi-tiered system of supports (CO MTSS)*. Retrieved from https://www.cde.state.co.us/mtss/ols-co-mtss-brochure2016

Committee for Children. (2016). *MindYeti*™ [Mobile application software]. Retrieved from https://www.mindyeti.com

Copeland, W. E., Keeler, G., Angold, A., & Costello, E. J. (2007). Traumatic events and posttraumatic stress in childhood. *Archives of General Psychiatry, 64*, 577–584. http://dx.doi.org/10.1001/archpsyc.64.5.577

Costello, E. J., Erkanli, A., Fairbank, J. A., & Angold, A. (2002). The prevalence of potentially traumatic events in childhood and adolescence. *Journal of Traumatic Stress, 15*, 99–112. http://dx.doi.org/10.1023/A:1014851823163

Coulton, C. J., Korbin, J. E., Su, M., & Chow, J. (1995). Community level factors and child maltreatment rates. *Child Development, 66*, 1262–1276. http://dx.doi.org/10.2307/1131646

Courtois, C. A., & Gold, S. N. (2009). The need for inclusion of psychological trauma in the professional curriculum: A call to action. *Psychological Trauma: Theory, Research, Practice, and Policy, 1*, 3–23.

Crouch, J. L., Hanson, R. F., Saunders, B. E., Kilpatrick, D. G., & Resnick, H. S. (2000). Income, race/ethnicity, and exposure to violence in youth: Results from the

National Survey of Adolescents. *Journal of Community Psychology, 28,* 625–641. http://dx.doi.org/10.1002/1520-6629(200011)28:6<625::AID-JCOP6>3.0.CO;2-R

Davis, R. G., Ressler, K. J., Schwartz, A. C., Stephens, K. J., & Bradley, R. G. (2008). Treatment barriers for low-income, urban African Americans with undiagnosed posttraumatic stress disorder. *Journal of Traumatic Stress, 21,* 218–222. http://dx.doi.org/10.1002/jts.20313

De Arellano, M. A., Waldrop, A. E., Deblinger, E., Cohen, J. A., Danielson, C. K., & Mannarino, A. R. (2005). Community outreach program for child victims of traumatic events: A community-based project for underserved populations. *Behavior Modification, 29,* 130–155. http://dx.doi.org/10.1177/0145445504270878

De Bellis, M. D., & Zisk, A. (2014). The biological effects of childhood trauma. *Child and Adolescent Psychiatric Clinics of North America, 23,* 185–222. http://dx.doi.org/10.1016/j.chc.2014.01.002

Delaney-Black, V., Covington, C., Ondersma, S. J., Nordstrom-Klee, B., Templin, T., Ager, J., . . . Sokol, R. J. (2002). Violence exposure, trauma, and IQ and/or reading deficits among urban children. *Archives of Pediatrics & Adolescent Medicine, 156,* 280–285. http://dx.doi.org/10.1001/archpedi.156.3.280

De Los Reyes, A., & Kazdin, A. E. (2005). Informant discrepancies in the assessment of childhood psychopathology: A critical review, theoretical framework, and recommendations for further study. *Psychological Bulletin, 131,* 483–509. http://dx.doi.org/10.1037/0033-2909.131.4.483

DeNavas-Walt, C., & Proctor, B. D. (2015). *Current population reports, P60-252: Income and poverty in the United States: 2014.* Washington, DC: U.S. Government Printing Office.

DePrince, A. P., & Newman, E. (2011). The art and science of trauma-focused training and education. *Psychological Trauma: Theory, Research, Practice, and Policy, 3,* 13–14.

DePrince, A. P., Weinzierl, K. M., & Combs, M. D. (2009). Executive function performance and trauma exposure in a community sample of children. *Child Abuse & Neglect, 33,* 353–361. http://dx.doi.org/10.1016/j.chiabu.2008.08.002

DeRosa, R., & Pelcovitz, D. (2009). Group treatment for chronically traumatized adolescents: Igniting SPARCS of change. In D. Brom, R. Pat-Horenczyk, & J. D. Ford (Eds.), *Treating traumatized children: Risk, resilience and recovery* (pp. 225–239). New York, NY: Routledge.

Dorado, J. S., Martinez, M., McArthur, L. E., & Leibovitz, T. (2016). Healthy Environments and Response to Trauma in Schools (HEARTS): A whole-school, multi-level, prevention and intervention program for creating trauma-informed, safe and supportive schools. *School Mental Health, 8,* 163–176. http://dx.doi.org/10.1007/s12310-016-9177-0

Durlak, J. A., Weissberg, R. P., Dymnicki, A. B., Taylor, R. D., & Schellinger, K. B. (2011). The impact of enhancing students' social and emotional learning: A meta-analysis of school-based universal interventions. *Child Development, 82,* 405–432. http://dx.doi.org/10.1111/j.1467-8624.2010.01564.x

Durso, L. E., & Gates, G. J. (2012). *Serving our youth: Findings from a national survey of service providers working with lesbian, gay, bisexual, and transgender youth who are homeless or at risk of becoming homeless.* Los Angeles, CA: The Williams Institute with True Colors Fund and The Palette Fund.

Elias, M. (2014). *Connecting SEL and the common core, Part one.* Retrieved from http://www.edutopia.org/blog/connecting-sel-and-common-core-part-one-maurice-elias

Evans, G. W. (2004). The environment of childhood poverty. *American Psychologist, 59,* 77–92. http://dx.doi.org/10.1037/0003-066X.59.2.77

Evans, S. W., Glass-Siegel, M., Frank, A., Van Treuren, R., Lever, N. A., & Weist, M. D. (2003). Overcoming the challenges of funding school mental health programs. In M. D. Weist, S. W. Evans, & N. A. Lever (Eds.), *Handbook of school mental health: Advancing practice and research* (pp. 73–86). New York, NY: Kluwer Academic. http://dx.doi.org/10.1007/978-0-387-73313-5_6

Family Educational Rights and Privacy Act of 1974, 20 U.S.C. § 1232g (1974).

Farmer, E. M. Z., Stangl, D. K., Burns, B. J., Costello, E. J., & Angold, A. (1999). Use, persistence, and intensity: Patterns of care for children's mental health across one year. *Community Mental Health Journal, 35*(1), 31–46. http://dx.doi.org/10.1023/A:1018743908617

Felitti, V. J., Anda, R. F., Nordenberg, D., Williamson, D. F., Spitz, A. M., Edwards, V., . . . Marks, J. S. (1998). Relationship of childhood abuse and household dysfunction to many of the leading causes of death in adults: The Adverse Childhood Experiences (ACE) Study. *American Journal of Preventive Medicine, 14,* 245–258. http://dx.doi.org/10.1016/S0749-3797(98)00017-8

Figley, C. R. (1995). *Compassion fatigue: Coping with secondary traumatic stress disorder in those who treat the traumatized.* New York, NY: Brunner/Mazel.

Finkelhor, D., Turner, H. A., Hamby, S. L., & Ormrod, R. K. (2011). Polyvictimization: Children's exposure to multiple types of violence, crime, and abuse. *OJJDP Juvenile Justice Bulletin* (NCJ235504, pp. 1–12). Washington, DC: U.S. Government Printing Office. Retrieved from https://www.ncjrs.gov/pdffiles1/ojjdp/235504.pdf

Finkelhor, D., Turner, H. A., Shattuck, A., & Hamby, S. L. (2015). Prevalence of childhood exposure to violence, crime, and abuse: Results from the National Survey of Children's Exposure to Violence. *JAMA Pediatrics, 169,* 746–754. http://dx.doi.org/10.1001/jamapediatrics.2015.0676

Flannery, D. J., Wester, K. L., & Singer, M. I. (2004). Impact of exposure to violence in school on child and adolescent mental health and behavior. *Journal of Community Psychology, 32*, 559–573. http://dx.doi.org/10.1002/jcop.20019

Fletcher, J. M., & Vaughn, S. (2009). Response to intervention: Preventing and remediating academic difficulties. *Child Development Perspectives, 3*, 30–37. http://dx.doi.org/10.1111/j.1750-8606.2008.00072.x

Foa, E. B., Johnson, K. M., Feeny, N. C., & Treadwell, K. R. (2001). The Child PTSD Symptom Scale: A preliminary examination of its psychometric properties. *Journal of Clinical Child Psychology, 30*, 376–384. http://dx.doi.org/10.1207/S15374424JCCP3003_9

Foa, E. B., Keane, T., Friedman, M. J., & Cohen, J. A. (Eds.). (2008). *Effective treatments for PTSD: Practice guidelines from the International Society of Traumatic Stress Studies.* New York, NY: Guilford Press.

Ford, J., Mahoney, K., & Russo, E. (2001). *TARGET and FREEDOM (for children).* Farmington: University of Connecticut Health Center.

Ford, J. D., Racusin, R., Ellis, C. G., Daviss, W. B., Reiser, J., Fleischer, A., & Thomas, J. (2000). Child maltreatment, other trauma exposure, and posttraumatic symptomatology among children with oppositional defiant and attention deficit hyperactivity disorders. *Child Maltreatment, 5*, 205–217. http://dx.doi.org/10.1177/1077559500005003001

Garbarino, J. (1995). The American war zone: What children can tell us about living with violence. *Journal of Developmental and Behavioral Pediatrics, 16*, 431–435. http://dx.doi.org/10.1097/00004703-199512000-00008

Garrison, E. G., Roy, I. S., & Azar, V. (1999). Responding to the mental health needs of Latino children and families through school-based services. *Clinical Psychology Review, 19*, 199–219.

Gelkopf, M., & Berger, R. (2009). A school-based, teacher-mediated prevention program (ERASE-Stress) for reducing terror-related traumatic reactions in Israeli youth: A quasi-randomized controlled trial. *Journal of Child Psychology and Psychiatry, 50*, 962–971. http://dx.doi.org/10.1111/j.1469-7610.2008.02021.x

Gillihan, S. J., Aderka, I. M., Conklin, P. H., Capaldi, S., & Foa, E. B. (2013). The Child PTSD Symptom Scale: Psychometric properties in female adolescent sexual assault survivors. *Psychological Assessment, 25*(1), 23–31. http://dx.doi.org/10.1037/a0029553

Goenjian, A. K., Karayan, I., Pynoos, R. S., Minassian, D., Najarian, L. M., Steinberg, A. M., & Fairbanks, L. A. (1997). Outcome of psychotherapy among early adolescents after trauma. *The American Journal of Psychiatry, 154*, 536–542.

Goenjian, A. K., Walling, D., Steinberg, A. M., Karayan, I., Najarian, L. M., & Pynoos, R. (2005). A prospective study of posttraumatic stress and depressive reactions among treated and untreated adolescents 5 years after a catastrophic disaster.

The American Journal of Psychiatry, 162, 2302–2308. http://dx.doi.org/10.1176/appi.ajp.162.12.2302

Gola, J. A., Beidas, R. S., Antinoro-Burke, D., Kratz, H. E., & Fingerhut, R. (2016). Ethical considerations in exposure therapy with children. *Cognitive and Behavioral Practice, 23*, 184–193. http://dx.doi.org/10.1016/j.cbpra.2015.04.003

Gonzalez, A., Monzon, N., Solis, D., Jaycox, L. H., & Langley, A. (2016). Trauma exposure in elementary school children: Description of screening procedures, level of exposure, and posttraumatic stress symptoms. *School Mental Health, 8*, 77–88.

Goodman, R. (1997). The Strengths and Difficulties Questionnaire: A research note. *Journal of Child Psychology and Psychiatry, 38*, 581–586. http://dx.doi.org/10.1111/j.1469-7610.1997.tb01545.x

Goodman, R., Meltzer, H., & Bailey, V. (1998). The Strengths and Difficulties Questionnaire: A pilot study on the validity of the self-report version. *European Child & Adolescent Psychiatry, 7*(3), 125–130. http://dx.doi.org/10.1007/s007870050057

Graham-Bermann, S. A., & Seng, J. (2005). Violence exposure and traumatic stress symptoms as additional predictors of health problems in high-risk children. *The Journal of Pediatrics, 146*, 349–354. http://dx.doi.org/10.1016/j.jpeds.2004.10.065

Gross, D., Julion, W., & Fogg, L. (2001). What motivates participation and dropout among low-income urban families of color in a prevention intervention? *Family Relations: Interdisciplinary Journal of Applied Family Studies, 50*, 246–254. http://dx.doi.org/10.1111/j.1741-3729.2001.00246.x

Gudiño, O. G., Leonard, S., & Cloitre, M. (2016). STAIR-A for girls: A pilot study of a group for traumatized youth in an urban school setting. *Journal of Child & Adolescent Trauma, 9*, 67–79. http://dx.doi.org/10.1007/s40653-015-0061-0

Gunnar, M., & Quevedo, K. (2007). The neurobiology of stress and development. *Annual Review of Psychology, 58*, 145–173. http://dx.doi.org/10.1146/annurev.psych.58.110405.085605

Guterman, N. B., Hahm, H. C., & Cameron, M. (2002). Adolescent victimization and subsequent use of mental health counseling services. *Journal of Adolescent Health, 30*, 336–345. http://dx.doi.org/10.1016/S1054-139X(01)00406-2

Health Insurance Portability and Accountability Act of 1996, Pub. L. 104–191, 110 Stat. 1936, 1996 (enacted).

Holmbeck, G. N., Devine, K. A., & Bruno, E. F. (2010). Developmental issues and considerations in research and practice. In J. R. Weisz & A. E. Kazdin (Eds.), *Evidence-based psychotherapies for children and adolescents* (2nd ed., pp. 28–39). New York, NY: Guilford Press.

Horner, R. H., Sugai, G., Smolkowski, K., Eber, L., Nakasato, J., Todd, A. W., & Esperanza, J. (2009). A randomized, wait-list controlled effectiveness trial assessing school-wide positive behavior support in elementary schools. *Journal of Positive Behavior Interventions, 11,* 133–144. http://dx.doi.org/10.1177/1098300709332067

Hoven, C. W., Duarte, C. S., Lucas, C. P., Wu, P., Mandell, D. J., Goodwin, R. D., . . . Susser, E. (2005). Psychopathology among New York City public school children 6 months after September 11. *Archives of General Psychiatry, 62,* 545–552. http://dx.doi.org/10.1001/archpsyc.62.5.545

Illinois State Board of Education. (2016). *Illinois learning standards: Social/emotional learning (SEL).* Retrieved from https://www.isbe.net/Pages/Social-Emotional-Learning-Standards.aspx

Individuals With Disabilities Education Improvement Act of 2004, 20 U.S.C.§ 1400 et seq. (2004).

Jaycox, L. H. (2003). *Cognitive behavioral intervention for trauma in schools.* Longmont, CO: Sopris West Educational Services.

Jaycox, L. H., Cohen, J. A., Mannarino, A. P., Walker, D. W., Langley, A. K., Gegenheimer, K. L., . . . Schonlau, M. (2010). Children's mental health care following Hurricane Katrina: A field trial of trauma-focused psychotherapies. *Journal of Traumatic Stress, 23,* 223–231.

Jaycox, L. H., Kataoka, S. H., Stein, B. D., Langley, A. K., & Wong, M. (2012). Cognitive-behavioral intervention for trauma in schools. *Journal of Applied School Psychology, 28,* 239–255. http://dx.doi.org/10.1080/15377903.2012.695766

Jaycox, L. H., Langley, A. K., & Dean, K. L. (2009). *Support for Students Exposed to Trauma: The SSET Program. Lesson plans, worksheets, and materials* (TR-675). Santa Monica, CA: RAND Corporation. Retrieved from http://www.rand.org/pubs/technical_reports/TR675/

Jaycox, L. H., Langley, A. K., Stein, B. D., Kataoka, S. H., & Wong, M. (2014). Early intervention for abused children in the school setting. In R. M. Reece, R. F. Hanson, & J. Sargent (Eds.), *Treatment of child abuse: Common ground for mental health, medical and legal practitioners* (2nd ed., pp. 76–85). Baltimore, MD: Johns Hopkins University Press.

Jaycox, L. H., Langley, A. K., Stein, B. D., Wong, M., Sharma, P., Scott, M., & Schonlau, M. (2009). Support for students exposed to trauma: A pilot study. *School Mental Health, 1,* 49–60. http://dx.doi.org/10.1007/s12310-009-9007-8

Jaycox, L. H., Morse, L. K., Tanielian, T., & Stein, B. D. (2006). *How schools can help students recover from traumatic experiences: A tool-kit for supporting long-term recovery* (Technical Report: TR-413). Santa Monica, CA: RAND Corporation. Retrieved from http://www.rand.org/pubs/technical_reports/TR413/

Jaycox, L. H., Stein, B. D., & Amaya-Jackson, L. M. (2008). School-based treatment for children and adolescents. In E. B. Foa, T. M. Keane, M. J. Friedman,

& J. A. Cohen (Eds.), *Effective treatments for PTSD: Practice guidelines from the International Society of Traumatic Stress Studies* (pp. 327–345). New York, NY: Guilford Press.

Jaycox, L. H., Stein, B. D., Amaya-Jackson, L. M., & Morse, L. K. (2007). School-based interventions for child traumatic stress. In S. W. Evans, M. Weist, & Z. Serpell (Eds.), *Advances in school-based mental health interventions* (Vol. 2, pp. 16-1–16-19). Kingston, NJ: Civic Research Institute.

Jaycox, L. H., Stein, B. D., Kataoka, S. H., Wong, M., Fink, A., Escudero, P., & Zaragoza, C. (2002). Violence exposure, posttraumatic stress disorder, and depressive symptoms among recent immigrant schoolchildren. *Journal of the American Academy of Child & Adolescent Psychiatry, 41*, 1104–1110. http://dx.doi.org/10.1097/00004583-200209000-00011

Jimerson, S. R., Burns, M. K., & VanDerHeyden, A. M. (2007). Response to intervention at school: The science and practice of assessment and intervention. In S. R. Jimerson, M. K. Burns, & A. M. VanDerHeyden (Eds.), *Handbook of response to intervention: The science and practice of assessment and intervention* (pp. 3–9). New York, NY: Springer. http://dx.doi.org/10.1007/978-0-387-49053-3_1

Kataoka, S., Jaycox, L. H., Wong, M., Nadeem, E., Langley, A., Tang, L., & Stein, B. D. (2011). Effects on school outcomes in low-income minority youth: Preliminary findings from a community-partnered study of a school-based trauma intervention. *Ethnicity & Disease, 21*(Suppl. 1), S1–S71.

Kataoka, S. H., Rowan, B., & Hoagwood, K. E. (2009). Bridging the divide: In search of common ground in mental health and education research and policy. *Psychiatric Services, 60*, 1510–1515. http://dx.doi.org/10.1176/ps.2009.60.11.1510

Kataoka, S. H., Stein, B. D., Jaycox, L. H., Wong, M., Escudero, P., Tu, W., . . . Fink, A. (2003). A school-based mental health program for traumatized Latino immigrant children. *Journal of the American Academy of Child & Adolescent Psychiatry, 42*, 311–318. http://dx.doi.org/10.1097/00004583-200303000-00011

Khamis, V., Macy, R., & Coignez, V. (2004). *Impact of the classroom/community/camp-based intervention program on Palestinian children.* USAID Report on Palestinian Children. Jerusalem: West Bank/Gaza Field Office, Save the Children USA.

Kilmer, R. P., Gil-Rivas, V., Griese, B., Hardy, S. J., Hafstad, G. S., & Alisic, E. (2014). Posttraumatic growth in children and youth: Clinical implications of an emerging research literature. *American Journal of Orthopsychiatry, 84*, 506–518. http://dx.doi.org/10.1037/ort0000016

Kilpatrick, D. G., Ruggiero, K. J., Acierno, R., Saunders, B. E., Resnick, H. S., & Best, C. L. (2003). Violence and risk of PTSD, major depression, substance abuse/dependence, and comorbidity: Results from the National Survey of

Adolescents. *Journal of Consulting and Clinical Psychology, 71,* 692–700. http://dx.doi.org/10.1037/0022-006X.71.4.692

Kira, I., Lewandowski, L., Somers, C. L., Yoon, J. S., & Chiodo, L. (2012). The effects of trauma types, cumulative trauma, and PTSD on IQ in two highly traumatized adolescent groups. *Psychological Trauma: Theory, Research, Practice, and Policy, 4,* 128–139. http://dx.doi.org/10.1037/a0022121

Kosciw, J. G. (2004). *The 2003 National School Climate Survey: The school-related experiences of our nation's lesbian, gay, bisexual, and transgender youth.* New York, NY: GLSEN.

Kovacs, M. (1985). The Children's Depression Inventory (CDI). *Psychopharmacology Bulletin, 21,* 995–998.

Langley, A., Santiago, C. D., Rodríguez, A., & Zelaya, J. (2013). Improving implementation of mental health services for trauma in multicultural elementary schools: Stakeholder perspectives on parent and educator engagement. *The Journal of Behavioral Health Services & Research, 40,* 247–262. http://dx.doi.org/10.1007/s11414-013-9330-6

Langley, A. K., Cohen, J. A., Mannarino, A. P., Jaycox, L. H., Schonlau, M., Scott, M., ... Gegenheimer, K. L. (2013). Trauma exposure and mental health problems among school children 15-months post-Hurricane Katrina. *Journal of Child & Adolescent Trauma, 6,* 143–156. http://dx.doi.org/10.1080/19361521.2013.812171

Langley, A. K., Gonzalez, A., Sugar, C. A., Solis, D., & Jaycox, L. (2015). Bounce Back: Effectiveness of an elementary school-based intervention for multicultural children exposed to traumatic events. *Journal of Consulting and Clinical Psychology, 83,* 853–865. http://dx.doi.org/10.1037/ccp0000051

Langley, A. K., Nadeem, E., Kataoka, S. H., Stein, B. D., & Jaycox, L. H. (2010). Evidence-based mental health programs in schools: Barriers and facilitators of successful implementation. *School Mental Health, 2,* 105–113. http://dx.doi.org/10.1007/s12310-010-9038-1

Layne, C. M., Pynoos, R. S., & Cardenas, J. (2001). Wounded adolescence: School-based group psychotherapy for adolescents who sustained or witnessed violent injury. In M. Shafii & S. Shafii (Eds.), *School violence: Contributing factors, management, and prevention* (pp. 163–180). Washington, DC: American Psychiatric Publishing, Inc.

Layne, C. M., Pynoos, R. S., Saltzman, W. R., Arslanagic, B., Black, M., Savjak, N., ... Houston, R. (2001). Trauma/grief-focused group psychotherapy: School-based postwar intervention with traumatized Bosnian adolescents. *Group Dynamics: Theory, Research, and Practice, 5,* 277–290. http://dx.doi.org/10.1037/1089-2699.5.4.277

Layne, C. M., Saltzman, W. R., Poppleton, L., Burlingame, G. M., Pasalić, A., Duraković, E., ... Pynoos, R. S. (2008). Effectiveness of a school-based group psychotherapy program for war-exposed adolescents: A randomized controlled trial. *Journal of the American Academy of Child and Adolescent Psychiatry, 47,* 1048–1062. http://dx.doi.org/10.1097/CHI.0b013e31817eecae

Leaf, P. J., & Keys, S. G. (2005). Collaborating for violence prevention: Training health professionals to work with schools. *American Journal of Preventive Medicine, 29*(Suppl. 2), 279–287. http://dx.doi.org/10.1016/j.amepre.2005.08.032

Lieberman, A. F., Van Horn, P., & Ippen, C. G. (2005). Toward evidence-based treatment: Child–parent psychotherapy with preschoolers exposed to marital violence. *Journal of the American Academy of Child & Adolescent Psychiatry, 44,* 1241–1248. http://dx.doi.org/10.1097/01.chi.0000181047.59702.58

Linehan, M. M. (1993). *Cognitive-behavioral treatment of borderline personality disorder.* New York, NY: Guilford Press.

Lynch, M. (2003). Consequences of children's exposure to community violence. *Clinical Child and Family Psychology Review, 6,* 265–274. http://dx.doi.org/10.1023/B:CCFP.0000006293.77143.e1

Macy, R. D. (2003). Community-based trauma response for youth. *New Directions for Youth Development: Theory, Practice, Research, 98,* 29–49. http://dx.doi.org/10.1002/yd.43

Macy, R. D., Bary, S., & Noam, G. G. (Eds.). (2003). Youth facing threat and terror supporting preparedness and resilience. *New directions for youth development* (No. 98, pp. 51–79). Indianapolis, IN: Jossey-Bass.

March, J. S., Amaya-Jackson, L., Murray, M. C., & Schulte, A. (1998). Cognitive-behavioral psychotherapy for children and adolescents with posttraumatic stress disorder after a single-incident stressor. *Journal of the American Academy of Child & Adolescent Psychiatry, 37,* 585–593. http://dx.doi.org/10.1097/00004583-199806000-00008

McKay, M. M., & Bannon, W. M., Jr. (2004). Engaging families in child mental health services. *Child and Adolescent Psychiatric Clinics of North America, 13,* 905–921. http://dx.doi.org/10.1016/j.chc.2004.04.001

McKay, M. M., McCadam, K., & Gonzales, J. J. (1996). Addressing the barriers to mental health services for inner city children and their caretakers. *Community Mental Health Journal, 32,* 353–361. http://dx.doi.org/10.1007/BF02249453

McLaughlin, K. A., Koenen, K. C., Hill, E. D., Petukhova, M., Sampson, N. A., Zaslavsky, A. M., & Kessler, R. C. (2013). Trauma exposure and posttraumatic stress disorder in a national sample of adolescents. *Journal of the American Academy of Child & Adolescent Psychiatry, 52,* 815–830.e14. http://dx.doi.org/10.1016/j.jaac.2013.05.011

Mohammad, E. T., Shapiro, E. R., Wainwright, L. D., & Carter, A. S. (2015). Impacts of family and community violence exposure on child coping and mental health.

Journal of Abnormal Child Psychology, 43, 203–215. http://dx.doi.org/10.1007/s10802-014-9889-2

Morgan, E., Salomon, N., Plotkin, M., & Cohen, R. (2014). *The school discipline consensus report: Strategies for the field to keep students engaged in school and out of the juvenile justice system.* New York, NY: The Council of State Governments Justice Center.

National Center for Telehealth and Technology. (2017). *Breathe2Relax* (Version 1.2) [Mobile application software]. Retrieved from http://t2health.dcoe.mil/apps/breathe2relax

National Child Traumatic Stress Network. (2008). *Child trauma toolkit for educators.* Retrieved from http://www.nctsn.org/resources/audiences/school-personnel/trauma-toolkit

National Child Traumatic Stress Network, National Center for PTSD. (2006). *Psychological first aid: Field operations guide* (2nd ed.). Retrieved from http://www.nctsn.org/sites/default/files/pfa/english/2-psyfirstaid_final_no_handouts.pdf

National Child Traumatic Stress Network, Secondary Traumatic Stress Committee. (2011). *Secondary traumatic stress: A fact sheet for child-serving professionals.* Los Angeles, CA, and Durham, NC: National Center for Child Traumatic Stress.

National Child Traumatic Stress Network, Secondary Traumatic Stress Committee. (2016). *Secondary traumatic stress: A fact sheet for organizations employing community violence workers.* Los Angeles, CA, and Durham, NC: National Center for Child Traumatic Stress.

National Governors Association Center for Best Practices, Council of Chief State School Officers. (2010). *Common core state standards.* Washington, DC: Author.

Nock, M. K., & Ferriter, C. (2005). Parent management of attendance and adherence in child and adolescent therapy: A conceptual and empirical review. *Clinical Child and Family Psychology Review, 8*, 149–166. http://dx.doi.org/10.1007/s10567-005-4753-0

Office of Special Education Programs Technical Assistance Center for Positive Behavioral Interventions and Support. (2016). *Multi-tiered Systems of Support (MTSS) & PBIS.* Retrieved from http://www.pbis.org/school/mtss

Olin, S. C., & Hoagwood, K. (2002). The Surgeon General's national action agenda on children's mental health. *Current Psychiatry Reports, 4*(2), 101–107. http://dx.doi.org/10.1007/s11920-002-0042-5

Oswald, D. P., Coutinho, M. J., Best, A. M., & Singh, N. N. (1999). Ethnic representation in special education: The influence of school-related economic and demographic variables. *The Journal of Special Education, 32*, 194–206. http://dx.doi.org/10.1177/002246699903200401

Overstreet, S., & Mathews, T. (2011). Challenges associated with exposure to chronic trauma: Using a public health framework to foster resilient outcomes among youth. *Psychology in the Schools, 48*, 738–754. http://dx.doi.org/10.1002/pits.20584

Owens, P. L., Hoagwood, K., Horwitz, S. M., Leaf, P. J., Poduska, J. M., Kellam, S. G., & Ialongo, N. S. (2002). Barriers to children's mental health services. *Journal of the American Academy of Child & Adolescent Psychiatry, 41*, 731–738. http://dx.doi.org/10.1097/00004583-200206000-00013

Perfect, M. M., & Morris, R. J. (2011). Delivering school-based mental health services by school psychologists: Education, training, and ethical issues. *Psychology in the Schools, 48*, 1049–1063. http://dx.doi.org/10.1002/pits.20612

Perfect, M. M., Turley, M. R., Carlson, J. S., Yohanna, J., & Pfenninger Saint Gilles, M. (2016). School-related outcomes of traumatic event exposure and traumatic stress symptoms in students: A systematic review of research from 1990 to 2015. *School Mental Health, 8*, 7–43. http://dx.doi.org/10.1007/s12310-016-9175-2

Perry, B. D. [The ChildTrauma Academy]. (2013, September 6). *The human brain* [Video file]. Retrieved from https://www.youtube.com/watch?v=uOsgDkeH52o

Perry, D. L., & Daniels, M. L. (2016). Implementing trauma-informed practices in the school setting: A pilot study. *School Mental Health, 8*, 177–188. http://dx.doi.org/10.1007/s12310-016-9182-3

Perzow, S. E., Petrenko, C. L., Garrido, E. F., Combs, M. D., Culhane, S. E., & Taussig, H. N. (2013). Dissociative symptoms and academic functioning in maltreated children: A preliminary study. *Journal of Trauma & Dissociation, 14*, 302–311. http://dx.doi.org/10.1080/15299732.2012.736928

Porche, M. V., Costello, D. M., & Rosen-Reynoso, M. (2016). Adverse family experiences, child mental health, and educational outcomes for a national sample of students. *School Mental Health, 8*, 44–60. http://dx.doi.org/10.1007/s12310-016-9174-3

Pumariega, A. J., Rothe, E., & Pumariega, J. B. (2005). Mental health of immigrants and refugees. *Community Mental Health Journal, 41*, 581–597.

Pynoos, R., Rodriguez, N., Steinberg, A., Stuber, M., & Frederick, C. (1998). *The University of California at Los Angeles posttraumatic stress disorder reaction index (UCLA PTSD RI) for DSM–IV (Revision 1)*. Los Angeles: UCLA Trauma Psychiatry Program.

Rauch, S., & Foa, E. (2006). Emotional processing theory (EPT) and exposure therapy for PTSD. *Journal of Contemporary Psychotherapy, 36*(2), 61–65. http://dx.doi.org/10.1007/s10879-006-9008-y

Resmovits, J. (2015, October 1). Effects of trauma could constitute disability, judge rules in Compton Unified case. *Los Angeles Times*. Retrieved from http://www.latimes.com/local/education/community/la-me-edu-compton-unified-trauma-could-constitute-disability-judge-20150930-story.html

Roberts, A. L., Rosario, M., Corliss, H. L., Koenen, K. C., & Austin, S. B. (2012). Elevated risk of posttraumatic stress in sexual minority youths: Mediation by childhood abuse and gender nonconformity. *American Journal of Public Health*, *102*, 1587–1593.

Rolfsnes, E. S., & Idsoe, T. (2011). School-based intervention programs for PTSD symptoms: A review and meta-analysis. *Journal of Traumatic Stress*, *24*, 155–165. http://dx.doi.org/10.1002/jts.20622

Saakvitne, K. W., Pearlman, L. A., & Staff of TSI/CAAP. (1996). *Transforming the pain: A workbook on vicarious traumatization*. New York, NY: Norton.

Saltzman, W. R., Pynoos, R. S., Layne, C. M., Steinberg, A. M., & Aisenberg, E. (2001). Trauma- and grief-focused intervention for adolescents exposed to community violence: Results of a school-based screening and group treatment protocol. *Group Dynamics: Theory, Research, and Practice*, *5*, 291–303. http://dx.doi.org/10.1037/1089-2699.5.4.291

Saltzman, W. R., Steinberg, A. M., Layne, C. M., Aisenberg, E., & Pynoos, R. S. (2001). A developmental approach to school-based treatment of adolescents exposed to trauma and traumatic loss. *Journal of Child & Adolescent Group Therapy*, *11*, 43–56. http://dx.doi.org/10.1023/A:1014789630162

Santiago, C. D., Fuller, A. K., Lennon, J. M., & Kataoka, S. H. (2016). Parent perspectives from participating in a family component for CBITS: Acceptability of a culturally informed school-based program. *Psychological Trauma: Theory, Research, Practice, and Policy*, *8*, 325–333. http://dx.doi.org/10.1037/tra0000076

Santiago, C. D., Kataoka, S. H., Hu-Cordova, M., Alvarado-Goldberg, K., Maher, L. M., & Escudero, P. (2015). Preliminary evaluation of a family treatment component to augment a school-based intervention serving low-income families. *Journal of Emotional and Behavioral Disorders*, *23*(1), 28–39. http://dx.doi.org/10.1177/1063426613503497

Santiago, C. D., Lennon, J. M., Fuller, A. K., Brewer, S. K., & Kataoka, S. H. (2014). Examining the impact of a family treatment component for CBITS: When and for whom is it helpful? *Journal of Family Psychology*, *28*, 560–570. http://dx.doi.org/10.1037/a0037329

Santiago, C. D., Pears, G., Baweja, S., Vona, P., Tang, J., & Kataoka, S. H. (2013). Engaging parents in evidence-based treatments in schools: Community perspectives from implementing CBITS. *School Mental Health*, *5*, 209–220. http://dx.doi.org/10.1007/s12310-012-9100-2

Santiago, C. D., Raviv, T., Ros, A. M., Brewer, S. K., Distel, L. M., Torres, S. A., . . . Langley, A. (in press). Implementing the Bounce Back trauma intervention in urban elementary schools: A real-world replication trial. *School Psychology Quarterly.*

Scheeringa, M. S. (2005). *Disaster experiences questionnaire* (Unpublished measure). Tulane University, New Orleans, LA.

Schreiber, M., Gurwitch, R., & Wong, M. (2006). *Listen, protect, connect—Model & teach: Psychological first aid (PFA) for students and teachers.* Washington, DC: U.S. Department of Homeland Security.

Shalev, I., Entringer, S., Wadhwa, P. D., Wolkowitz, O. M., Puterman, E., & Epel, E. S. (2013). Stress and telomere biology: A lifespan perspective. *Psychoneuroendocrinology, 38,* 1835–1842.

Sharkey, P. (2010). The acute effect of local homicides on children's cognitive performance. *PNAS Proceedings of the National Academy of Sciences of the United States of America, 107,* 11733–11738. http://dx.doi.org/10.1073/pnas.1000690107

Singer, B., Ryff, C. D., Carr, D., & Magee, W. J. (1998). Linking life histories and mental health: A person-centered strategy. *Sociological Methodology, 28*(1), 1–51. http://dx.doi.org/10.1111/0081-1750.00041

Singer, M. I., Anglin, T. M., Song, L.Y., & Lunghofer, L. (1995). Adolescents' exposure to violence and associated symptoms of psychological trauma. *JAMA, 273,* 477–482.

Snell-Johns, J., Mendez, J. L., & Smith, B. H. (2004). Evidence-based solutions for overcoming access barriers, decreasing attrition, and promoting change with underserved families. *Journal of Family Psychology, 18,* 19–35. http://dx.doi.org/10.1037/0893-3200.18.1.19

Stein, B. D., Jaycox, L. H., Kataoka, S. H., Wong, M., Tu, W., Elliott, M. N., & Fink, A. (2003). A mental health intervention for schoolchildren exposed to violence: A randomized controlled trial. *JAMA: Journal of the American Medical Association, 290,* 603–611. http://dx.doi.org/10.1001/jama.290.5.603

Stephan, S. H., Sugai, G., Lever, N., & Connors, E. (2015). Strategies for integrating mental health into schools via a multitiered system of support. *Child and Adolescent Psychiatric Clinics of North America, 24,* 211–231. http://dx.doi.org/10.1016/j.chc.2014.12.002

Stevens, J., Kelleher, K. J., Ward-Estes, J., & Hayes, J. (2006). Perceived barriers to treatment and psychotherapy attendance in child community mental health centers. *Community Mental Health Journal, 42,* 449–458. http://dx.doi.org/10.1007/s10597-006-9048-5

Straussner, J. H., & Straussner, S. L. (1997). Impact of community school violence on children. In N. K. Phillips & S. L. A. Straussner (Eds.), *Children in the urban environment: Linking social policy and clinical practice* (pp. 61–77). Springfield, IL: Charles C Thomas.

Substance Abuse and Mental Health Services Administration. (2014). *SAMHSA's concept of trauma and guidance for a trauma-informed approach* (Health and Human Services Publication No. 14-4884). Rockville, MD: Author.

Sullivan, P. M., & Knutson, J. F. (2000). Maltreatment and disabilities: A population-based epidemiological study. *Child Abuse & Neglect, 24,* 1257–1273. http://dx.doi.org/10.1016/S0145-2134(00)00190-3

Thapa, A., Cohen, J., Guffey, S., & Higgins-D'Alessandro, A. (2013). A review of school climate research. *Review of Educational Research, 83,* 357–385. Advance online publication. http://dx.doi.org/10.3102/0034654313483907

Turner, H. A., Finkelhor, D., & Ormrod, R. (2006). The effect of lifetime victimization on the mental health of children and adolescents. *Social Science & Medicine, 62,* 13–27. http://dx.doi.org/10.1016/j.socscimed.2005.05.030

Turner, H. A., Vanderminden, J., Finkelhor, D., Hamby, S., & Shattuck, A. (2011). Disability and victimization in a national sample of children and youth. *Child Maltreatment, 16,* 275–286. http://dx.doi.org/10.1177/1077559511427178

U.S. Department of Education, Office of Safe and Drug-Free Schools. (2007). *Practical information on crisis planning: A guide for schools and communities.* Washington, DC: Author.

U.S. Department of Health and Human Services. (2003). *New freedom commission on mental health, achieving the promise: Transforming mental health care in America. Final report* (SMA-03-3832). Rockville, MD: Author.

U.S. Public Health Service. (2000). *Report of the Surgeon General's Conference on Children's Mental Health: A national action agenda.* Washington, DC: Department of Health and Human Services.

Van Dernoot Lipsky, L. (2009). *Trauma stewardship: An everyday guide to caring for self while caring for others.* San Francisco, CA: Berrett-Koehler.

Vernberg, E. M., La Greca, A. M., Silverman, W. K., & Prinstein, M. J. (1996). Prediction of posttraumatic stress symptoms in children after Hurricane Andrew. *Journal of Abnormal Psychology, 105,* 237–248. http://dx.doi.org/10.1037/0021-843X.105.2.237

Ward, B., & Gersten, R. (2013). A randomized evaluation of the Safe and Civil Schools model for positive behavioral interventions and supports at elementary schools in a large urban district. *School Psychology Review, 42,* 317–333.

Weiss, H. B., Lopez, M. E., & Rosenberg, H. (2010). *Beyond random acts: Family, school, and community engagement as an integral part of education reform.* Harvard Family Research Project Report. Retrieved from http://www.hfrp.org/publications-resources/browse-our-publications/beyond-random-acts-family-school-and-community-engagement-as-an-integral-part-of-education-reform

Weissberg, R. P., & Cascarino, J. (2013). Academic learning + social-emotional learning = national priority. *Phi Delta Kappan, 95,* 8–13. http://dx.doi.org/10.1177/003172171309500203

Weist, M. D., Mellin, E. A., Chambers, K. L., Lever, N. A., Haber, D., & Blaber, C. (2012). Challenges to collaboration in school mental health and strategies for overcoming them. *The Journal of School Health, 82,* 97–105. http://dx.doi.org/10.1111/j.1746-1561.2011.00672.x

Weist, M. D., & Paternite, C. E. (2006). Building an interconnected policy-training-practice-research agenda to advance school mental health. *Education & Treatment of Children, 29,* 173–196.

Zakrzewski, V. (2014). *How to integrate social-emotional learning into common core.* Berkeley: Greater Good Science Center, University of California. Retrieved from http://greatergood.berkeley.edu/article/item/how_to_integrate_social_emotional_learning_into_common_core.

Index

About the Authors

Catherine DeCarlo Santiago, PhD, is a licensed clinical psychologist and an assistant professor of clinical psychology at Loyola University Chicago. Dr. Santiago specializes in community intervention research with children and families. She studies how children and families respond to stress and trauma and evaluates interventions designed to improve functioning and promote resilience. She has worked directly with the Cognitive Behavioral Intervention for Trauma in Schools (CBITS) team, conducting school-based intervention research, designing evaluations, and supervising clinicians who are implementing CBITS. Dr. Santiago has partnered with school-based clinicians, school administrators, and community parents to inform school-based interventions and improve their implementation and sustainability. She provides supervision and implementation support to graduate students and school-based clinicians. She received her bachelor of arts degree from the University of Notre Dame and a doctoral degree in clinical psychology from the University of Denver. Dr. Santiago completed her clinical internship and postdoctoral fellowship at the University of California, Los Angeles Semel Institute for Neuroscience and Human Behavior.

Tali Raviv, PhD, is a clinical psychologist at Ann and Robert H. Lurie Children's Hospital of Chicago and an assistant professor at Northwestern University Feinberg School of Medicine. She is part of the Center for

Childhood Resilience at Lurie Children's whose mission is to increase access to high-quality mental health services for youth affected by poverty, trauma, and violence by providing training and technical assistance to school- and community-based clinicians as well as educators and other youth-serving organizations. Dr. Raviv has trained hundreds of clinicians in school-based interventions to trauma, including Cognitive Behavioral Intervention for Trauma in Schools (CBITS) and Bounce Back, and hundreds of educators and community members on the impact that trauma has on students' learning and emotional and behavioral health. She has also worked directly with multiple schools on the creation and implementation of Behavioral Health Teams, school-based teams that meet to address the needs of at-risk students, including those affected by exposure to violence and trauma. She provides direct clinical services to youth and families exposed to trauma through her work on the Trauma Treatment Service at Lurie Children's Hospital, and participates in advocacy initiatives through membership in the Illinois Child Trauma Coalition and her role on the Steering Committee of the PATHH Collaborative of the Chicago Children's Advocacy Center. Dr. Raviv received her bachelor of arts degree from Emory University and her doctoral degree in clinical psychology from the University of Denver.

Lisa H. Jaycox, PhD, is a clinical psychologist and senior behavioral scientist at the RAND Corporation. Dr. Jaycox's work focuses on the mental health consequences of stress and trauma and on interventions that facilitate recovery. She has worked on the development and implementation of the Cognitive Behavioral Intervention for Trauma in Schools (CBITS) program and related interventions (Support for Students Exposed to Trauma, Bounce Back, Life Improvement for Teens) for more than 15 years, and she has conducted research on stress and a broad range of traumatic events in children and adults. After Hurricanes Katrina and Rita, she developed a toolkit for schools that described trauma-focused school interventions. Dr. Jaycox received her bachelor of arts degree from Brown University and her doctoral degree from the University of Pennsylvania.